**Michael Frayn** was born in London in 1933 and read Russian, French and Moral Sciences (Philosophy) at Emmanuel College, Cambridge. He began his career as a journalist on the *Manchester Guardian* and the *Observer*. His award-winning plays include *Alphabetical Order*, *Make and Break* and *Noises Off*, all of which received Best Comedy of the Year awards, while *Benefactors* was named Best Play of the Year. Two of his most recent plays, *Copenhagen* and *Democracy*, also won numerous awards (including, for *Copenhagen*, the Tony in New York and the Prix Molière in Paris). In 2006 *Donkeys' Years* was revived in the West End thirty years after its premiere and was followed in 2007 by his latest play, *The Crimson Hotel*. He has translated Chekhov's last four plays, dramatised a selection of his one-act plays and short stories under the title *The Sneeze*, and adapted his first, untitled play, as *Wild Honey*. His novels include *Towards the End of the Morning* (in the USA, *Against Entropy*), *The Trick of It*, *A Landing on the Sun*, *Headlong* and *Spies*. His most recent books are works of philosophy, *The Human Touch* and *Stage Directions: Writing on Theatre 1970–2008*. He is married to the biographer and critic Claire Tomalin.

*By the same author*

*Novels*
Headlong
A Landing on the Sun
Now You Know
The Russian Interpreter
Spies
Sweet Dreams
The Tin Men
Towards the End of the Morning
The Trick of It
A Very Private Life

*Plays*
Alphabetical Order
Audience
Balmoral
La Belle Vivette
Benefactors
Clockwise (*screenplay*)
Clouds
Copenhagen
The Crimson Hotel
Democracy
Donkeys' Years
First and Last (*screenplay*)
Here
Jamie on a Flying Visit & Birthday
Look Look
Make and Break
Noises Off
Now You Know
The Two of Us
Wild Honey

*Non-fiction*
Collected Columns
Constructions
The Human Touch
Stage Directions

*Translations*
The Cherry Orchard
Exchange
Fruits of Enlightenment
Number One
The Seagull
The Sneeze
Three Sisters
Uncle Vanya

**Michael Frayn**

# Afterlife

**Methuen Drama**

Published by Methuen Drama 2008

1 3 5 7 9 10 8 6 4 2

Methuen Drama
A & C Black Publishers Limited
38 Soho Square
London W1D 3HB
www.acblack.com

ISBN: 978 1 408 10833 8

A CIP catalogue record for this book is available from the British Library

Typeset by Country Setting, Kingsdown, Kent
Printed and bound in Great Britain by
CPI Cox & Wyman, Reading, RG1 8EX

### Caution

*Afterlife* was first presented in the Lyttelton auditorium of the National Theatre, London, on 11 June 2008. The cast was as follows:

| | |
|---|---|
| **Max Reinhardt** | Roger Allam |
| **Helene Thimig** | Abigail Cruttenden |
| **Gusti Adler** | Selina Griffiths |
| **Rudolf 'Katie' Kommer** | Peter Forbes |
| **Franz** | Glyn Grain |
| **The Prince Archbishop of Salzburg** | David Burke |
| **Friedrich Müller** | David Schofield |
| **Players** | Nicholas Lumley |
| | David Baron |
| | Colin Haigh |
| | Sarah Head |
| | Elizabeth Marsh |
| | Charlotte Melia |
| | Hugh Osborne |
| | Peter Prentice |
| | Claire Winsper |
| | Rupert Young |

*Director*   Michael Blakemore
*Set Designer*   Peter Davison
*Costume Designer*   Sue Willmington
*Lighting Designer*   Neil Austin
*Music and Sound Designer*   Paul Charlier

# Afterlife

**Characters**

**Max Reinhardt**
**Helene Thimig**, *his companion and then second wife*
**Gusti Adler**, *his personal assistant*
**Rudolf ('Katie') Kommer**, *his man of business*
**Franz**, *his valet*
**The Prince Archbishop of Salzburg**
**Friedrich Müller**, *a citizen of Salzburg*
**Thomas, Josef, Liesl, Gretl**, *and* **Others**

# Act One

*Stairs, levels, galleries.*

*Enter all: the* **Prince Archbishop**, **Thimig**, **Adler**, **Kommer**, **Müller**, **Thomas**, **Josef**, **Liesl**, **Gretl** *and* **Franz**.

**Reinhardt**
> Draw near, good people all, I pray!
> Give heed while we perform our play,
> Wherein we show, as best we can,
> The Summoning of Everyman.

And we stage it very simply. Here, if Your Grace should give us permission. On the square in front of the cathedral. Under the open sky. The way the old morality plays were done five centuries ago. Your Grace . . .

*He indicates a chair for the* **Prince Archbishop**.

**Reinhardt**   All of you . . .

**Thomas**, **Josef**, **Liesl**, **Gretl** *and* **Franz** *help* **Thimig**, **Adler**, **Kommer**, *and* **Müller** *to find places to sit, but themselves remain discreetly standing.*

**Reinhardt**   A few boards thrown across trestles for the actors to stand on. Boards and benches round the square for the audience. Nothing else. And we start in the afternoon. In the plain light of day. The doors of the cathedral are thrown open, the cast enters . . . The audience quietens and settles . . . The Prologue speaks . . .

> Here all shall learn, with eyes to see,
> How short our days on earth do be,
> How sorrowful must be our end,
> Should we our ways neglect to mend.
> Plain be the matter, plain our speech,
> And plain the lesson here that each
> May haply in our story find,
> And henceforth ever bear in mind . . .

Whereupon the play proper commences . . .

**Prince Archbishop**    Perhaps we might pause for one moment first, Herr Reinhardt.

**Reinhardt**    Your Grace.

**Prince Archbishop**    Let me make sure I understand exactly what I am to be presented with. I am of course very conscious of your reputation, and, I may say, impressed by your command of the text . . .

**Adler**    Herr Reinhardt always knows the whole play by heart before he begins.

**Reinhardt**    My personal assistant, Fräulein Adler.

**Adler**    He has the whole production in his head. All written down in his prompt-book. (*She shows him.*) Every inflexion, every gesture. Every pause, every breath.

**Thimig**    The sort of thing that actors usually hate. But Herr Reinhardt is an exception to all the rules.

**Reinhardt**    Fräulein Thimig, who is one of our cast.

**Prince Archbishop**    I have had the pleasure of seeing you perform in Vienna. Ophelia – yes? Most touching.

**Thimig**    Your Grace is very kind.

**Prince Archbishop**    So, Herr Reinhardt, let me be quite clear. This is a morality play? A play of a religious nature?

**Reinhardt**    A traditional English morality play. But freely adapted by Herr von Hofmannsthal.

**Prince Archbishop**    Herr von Hofmannsthal is a Jew?

**Reinhardt**    A Catholic, Your Grace.

**Kommer**    His grandfather was a Jew!

**Reinhardt**    Herr Kommer, my irrepressible man of business.

**Prince Archbishop**    Herr Kommer . . .

**Kommer**    Call me Katie, Your Grace. Everyone else does.

**Prince Archbishop**  Katie. Very well. Herr Katie? Or Frau Katie?

**Kommer**  Now, now, Your Grace!

**Prince Archbishop**  And you, Herr Reinhardt? A Jew?

**Reinhardt**  A Jew, Your Grace.

**Prince Archbishop**  A Jew. And you have chosen a work of Catholic piety to open your new festival?

**Kommer**  You want Jewish piety? In Salzburg? What else? Ice skating in hell?

**Reinhardt**  Thank you, Katie.

**Prince Archbishop**  And yet I believe your choice has so far found little favour in the city.

**Kommer**  You're our last hope!

**Prince Archbishop** (*to* **Reinhardt**)  Yes?

**Reinhardt**  Yes, Your Grace.

**Prince Archbishop**  As long as we know where we stand. So, let us hear the play, then, Herr Reinhardt.

**Reinhardt**  Your Grace. Suddenly . . . a voice comes down from heaven:

> Should I, who rule as God on high,
> Stand patiently for ever by
> While men on earth below ignore
> My dread command, and mock My law?
> While they on evil gorge and feast,
> More vile than e'en the lowliest beast?

**Prince Archbishop**  The Almighty?

**Reinhardt**  Indeed, Your Grace.

**Prince Archbishop**  And you have every gesture of the Almighty written down in your book?

*He holds out his hand for the prompt-book.* **Adler** *glances at* **Reinhardt**, *who nods. She hands the* **Prince Archbishop** *the book. He leafs slowly through it.*

**Reinhardt**   Indeed, Your Grace.

**Prince Archbishop**   Every inflexion? Every breath? Of the Lord God Himself?

**Reinhardt**   Your Grace, we find ourselves living in the year 1920, in an age when faith has been questioned, and it is difficult to speak of God without self-consciousness. But for a few short hours we shall relive the simple-hearted innocence of the fifteenth century, when God was as real and familiar as the local weaver and the local tinker and the local bellows-maker. Our cast will be highly skilled professional actors. But what they will be acting for us is *not* being professional actors. They will be not just God and Death and Everyman. They will be the local weaver and the local tinker and the local bellows-maker *playing* God and Death and Everyman. This is how the theatre allows us to explore God's creation. We all have possibilities in us that ordinary life won't let us realise. We all have only one birth and one death. We are all different, but in the narrow stream-bed of everyday life we are rolled together like pebbles until we all look alike. Or until we shake ourselves free and begin to act out the other parts that life denies us. And here, on the cathedral square in Salzburg, we shall do it as simply and naturally as children do in their games. No sound effects. Only the cathedral bells. Only the distant sound of traffic in the streets.

*Sound effects.*

Only the whirr of the pigeons' wings, as they swirl up and away like a sudden eddy of smoke from a bonfire.

*The sound of the pigeons. Everyone turns to follow them.*

Only the voice of God.

> Sunk deep in sin they know me not;
> That I am God they have forgot.
> And scant the care of aught they show
> Save worldly weal and worldly woe.

No lighting effects. Only the afternoon sunlight coming and going . . .

*The sunlight comes and goes.*

Only the words. Words, words, words. The old resource. The words and the weather. Chill flurries of wind off the mountains behind us . . . Rain at times, of course. This is a rainy town! Heavy rain and we run for cover . . .

*The **Prince Archbishop** studies the prompt-book. **Adler** and **Thimig** look at each other apprehensively.*

**Prince Archbishop** (*reads thoughtfully*)
They little mark what coin I paid,
What sacrifice for them I made.
To spare their feet from hidden thorn
I let instead my brow be torn.
All care I could of man I took –
Yet now by man am I forsook . . .

*He stops and considers. **Kommer** makes a thumbs-down to the others.*

**Prince Archbishop** (*stands, authoritatively*)
Therefore have I with sudden speed
A day of reckoning decreed,
When Everyman shall give at last
Account of all things, now and past.
Where art thou, Death, my strong right hand?
Come forth, approach. Before me stand.

**Reinhardt** (*as **Death***)
Thy will, Almighty God, convey;
Most punctually shall I obey.

**Prince Archbishop**
To Everyman I charge thee go.
In My name shalt thou make him know
He stands required to engage
Upon a solemn pilgrimage –
And that right soon, this very day.
Hear no excuse, brook no delay.
And let him bring his reckoning book

That I may open it and look
To see what rightful balance should
Be struck 'twixt evil deed and good.

**Reinhardt**
Like bolt from thundercloud I go
To seek out Everyman below.
Thy dread command will I make known,
And speed him hence before Thy throne.

**Prince Archbishop** (*hands the prompt-book back to* **Adler**)
Thank you.

**Thimig**    Bravo, Your Grace!

**Kommer**    Give him a contract!

**Prince Archbishop**    You were telling us, I believe, that we all have more possibilities in us than our everyday selves can encompass. Even as Archbishop of Salzburg –

**Kommer**    Prince Archbishop of Salzburg!

**Prince Archbishop**    Even as Prince Archbishop of Salzburg one has less opportunity than might be supposed to play God. No opportunity at all, really, to preside over the Day of Judgment.

**Kommer**    You're presiding over it now!

**Reinhardt**    Katie, Katie . . .

**Prince Archbishop**    So I am. Then let us continue. My good friend Death, I believe, is out scouring the streets of Salzburg for Everyman.

**Reinhardt**    There he goes. Up the Franziskanergasse, down the Judengasse . . . Past the Collegiate Church and the University . . . He looks into the beer-gardens and the coffee-houses, the hospitals and the night shelters . . . There . . . ! There . . . ! But you can't see him. He's just a passing breath of cold air, like the wind off the mountains. The only man who will ever see him is the one he is looking for. Everyman. And who is Everyman? It could be anyone. Someone with no suspicion of what's about to happen to him. Someone in the prime of life, perhaps, who's enjoying everything that the world can offer, and proud of it. Me. Your Grace. Death will know him when he sees him! Now, the scene changes. We are in front of a great house somewhere on the outskirts of the city.

**Prince Archbishop**   How will you manage that, Herr Reinhardt?

**Reinhardt**   We shall listen to the words. Yes? And use our imagination.

**Prince Archbishop**   Of course, of course.

**Reinhardt**   The doors open. We enter the lofty hall. And there in front of the great hearth stands . . .

**Prince Archbishop**   Everyman.

**Reinhardt**   Everyman.

> A lordly house I own and fair,
> Magnificent beyond compare.
> Full many a chamber call I mine
> With costly furnishings and fine . . .

**Liesl** *and* **Gretl** *set a few costly furnishings.*

**Reinhardt**
> Full many a chest with riches laden . . .

**Thomas** *and* **Josef** *carry in a large trunk.*

**Reinhardt**
> Full many a serving man and maiden.
> With precious plate my cupboards gleam,
> With good fat kine my pastures teem.
> And sweet the heavy harvest yield
> Of golden rent from every field.
> So I, untouched by care or sorrow,
> May smile today, and laugh tomorrow.

**Prince Archbishop**   This house you have conjured up, Herr Reinhardt . . . It looks remarkably like your own house!

**Kommer**   It *is* his own house!

**Reinhardt**   Welcome, Your Grace.

**Kommer**
Draw near, good people all, I pray!
Max Reinhardt is at home today!

**Thomas**, **Josef**, **Liesl** *and* **Gretl** *serve champagne and canapés.*

**Prince Archbishop**   And a famous house it is. One of our great baroque palaces!

**Reinhardt**   Built by one of our great baroque princes. Your illustrious predecessor. There he is.

**Prince Archbishop**   Twice life size. Hanging in the place of honour.

**Kommer**   He built this house – good! Chucked all the Protestants out of Salzburg – not so good!

**Reinhardt**   It was one of Your Grace's predecesssors, though, who helped to give Mozart his start in life.

**Kommer**   And another one had him kicked out on his behind. Great chuckers-out, you Prince Archbishops!

**Reinhardt**   This house. The music of Mozart. They were the legacy of your predecessors to future generations. Our play could be Your Grace's.

**Kommer**   Does everyone have a glass? Ladies and gentlemen – His Grace and Highness the Prince Archbishop of Salzburg!

**Everyone**   His Grace and Highness!

**Prince Archbishop**   Come, come. Simply 'His Grace'.

**Kommer**   So, Your Grace, what's the answer going to be? Yes or no?

**Prince Archbishop**   My word, though! Look at it! The great hall! The ceremonial staircase! The galleries!

**Reinhardt** Most of it in a woefully dilapidated state. It will be my life's work to restore it to what it once was.

**Kommer** If there's one thing Herr Reinhardt loves it's a lordly house! A wing of the Crown Prince's palace in Berlin. An apartment in the Emperor's palace in Vienna.

**Reinhardt** Merely *pieds-à-terre*. Now I have found Leopoldskron I intend to make this my home. I have a passion for the baroque, Your Grace. The baroque is the extension of the theatre into the everyday world. And that is what I have devoted my career to – breaking down the barriers between the actual and the imagined. Between art and life, between theatre and audience. And doing it as simply and naturally as children do in their games. A few props – pictures, footmen . . . and at once we're in the eighteenth century – in a play – in an opera – in a dream . . . I want to do it not just for the wealthy and the privileged few, sitting in some small room sealed off from the world, but out in the world itself, where popular drama began. So that all of us, princes and footmen alike, ladies and ladies' maids, can escape for a few brief hours from the life sentences we are serving inside our own selves.

**Prince Archbishop** Some of the local residents have not so far been as appreciative as you might have wished.

**Kommer** Everyman has the same trouble! Where's the book . . . ? Poor Neighbour. As soon as Everyman sets foot outside his house, up comes Poor Neighbour, hand out, pester pester . . .

**Reinhardt** Poor Neighbour. Will someone read Poor Neighbour . . . ?

**Müller** Poor Neighbour? I'll read Poor Neighbour!

*He takes the prompt-book from* **Adler**.

**Kommer** Who are *you*?

**Müller** No one. I live in Salzburg.

**Kommer** So what are you doing here?

**Müller**  Nothing. Out of work, like everyone else. Passing the time. Playing Poor Neighbour for you.

> I dwelt once in a house as fine
> Until my fortune's late decline . . .
> Now must I kneel to thee and plead
> For help in this my hour of need.

**Reinhardt**  Excellent. Most convincing. Thank you.

> To hear thy woes I cannot stay.
> Here – take this coin and go thy way.

*He fumbles in his pockets.*

**Adler**  Coin, someone? Cash?

**Kommer**  Herr Reinhardt's like royalty. Never soils his fingers with money.

*He gives **Reinhardt** a coin.*

**Reinhardt** (*passes the coin to **Müller***)
> Here – take this coin and go thy way.

**Müller**
> Hath God such meagre comfort sent me?

**Reinhardt**
> Meagre? Odd's teeth! I do repent me!

*He takes the coin back again, and gives it to **Kommer**.*

**Kommer**  Anything to do with money – me.

**Reinhardt**
> Thou – to my counting-house repair
> And fetch the bag of money there.

**Kommer**  You see?

> I run thy orders to obey –
> Already I am on my way.

**Reinhardt** (*to **Thomas**, **Josef**, **Liesl**, and **Gretl***)
> And you – go tell my cooks: 'Tonight
> I shall a hundred guests invite.'

A banquet let them conjure up
On which an emperor might sup:
The best of wine, the best of meat –
And more than any man can eat.

**Kommer** *returns and hands* **Reinhardt** *a bag.*

**Müller**
The gold thou hast in this one sack
Would more than furnish all I lack.
Some part of it I beg thee share –
Thou hast enough and more to spare.

**Reinhardt**
No groat of it that ever could
Become thine, even if I would.

*Takes the prompt-book back from* **Müller** *and hands it to* **Adler**.

**Reinhardt**
A pleasure garden have I bought
Whereto my mistress may resort.
This day am I obliged to go
And pay the balance that I owe.
The wealth thy envious eyes here see
In truth belongs no more to me.

**Kommer**    Nor to Herr Reinhardt! The gardens are soaking up as much as the house!

**Prince Archbishop**    The palace gardens – yes! You are restoring *them* to their former glory?

**Reinhardt**    More than restoring them. I am making plans beyond even what your great predecessor ever imagined.

*Shows him the view.*

**Kommer**    Lakeside terraces and walks – fountains – a menagerie – an open-air theatre . . .

**Prince Archbishop**    And such serenity . . . The last of the day's light reflected in the lake . . . The profound blue stillness of the mountains beyond . . .

**Reinhardt**   I love this time of day, Your Grace. Twilight . . . It's where I have spent my life. In the border lands between the hard light of day and the ghosts of night. Smuggling whatever I could across the uncertain frontier between reality and dream.

**Prince Archbishop**   What about the frontier we're looking at up there in the mountains, Herr Reinhardt? Your greatest triumphs were on the other side of it, were they not?

**Reinhardt**   The frontier between Austria and Germany is the frontier between past and present, Your Grace. Germany is behind me. I have come back to Austria. To my native land.

**Prince Archbishop**   You don't feel a little wistful, when you see the bright lights of Germany twinkling away up there?

**Reinhardt**   I have come home, Your Grace! In every sense . . .

**Thimig**   And Herr Reinhardt intends to make this house a home not just for himself, but for all the actors and artists who come to perform here.

**Adler**   Somewhere they can share a simple communal life together.

**Thimig**   A kind of artistic cloister.

**Kommer**   With Max Reinhardt as its abbot!

**Reinhardt**   I am restoring the old chapel. Perhaps it could be reconsecrated? I should welcome your advice.

**Prince Archbishop**   You Austrian Jews! If only all our Catholics took as much interest in the faith!

**Kommer**   We love it! Of course we love it! Baroque curlicues! Fugues and kyries! Wine and blood! Smoke, music, gorgeous dresses! Confessions! Curses! Murders! Deathbed repentances! – Pure theatre! We're all in the same line of business!

**Reinhardt**   Easier, perhaps, to be what one isn't than what one is. May I show you my plans, Your Grace . . . ?

*Exit* **Prince Archbishop** *and* **Adler**.

**Reinhardt** (*to* **Thomas, Josef, Liesl,** *and* **Gretl**)  Lanterns, candles!

*They exit.* **Thimig** *detains* **Reinhardt**

**Thimig** (*to* **Reinhardt**, *aside*)  He knows! About you and me! When you said about a pleasure garden for your mistress! He gave me a look!

**Kommer**  Everyone knows, my darling! Everyone knows!

**Thimig**  Not in Salzburg!

**Kommer**  No, or we'd be in even more trouble than we are.

*Exit* **Reinhardt, Thimig,** *and* **Kommer**.

**Müller** (*takes a canapé*)  So what's your name?

**Franz**  Franz, if you please, sir.

**Müller**  Franz . . . Franz what?

**Franz**  Just Franz, thank you, sir.

**Müller**  Herr Reinhardt's footman?

**Franz**  Herr Reinhardt's valet.

**Müller**  Oh yes. His famous valet. Sit down, Franz. Put your feet up. Have a canapé. You don't have to bother about me. I'm nobody.

**Franz** (*declines*)  Thank you, sir.

**Müller**  No? Well, as you please. (*Sits.*) Franz, yes. You were in service with the late Emperor's brother.

**Franz**  Sir.

**Müller**  Nothing but the best for Herr Reinhardt! Even his valet belonged to an Archduke. The lovely Luziwuzi. An Archduke and an Archduchess combined. Did you have to dress him on the days he was an Archduchess? Skirts, petticoats? Or did he have a lady's maid for his more feminine side?

**Franz**  More champagne, sir?

**Müller**   What a life we lead in Austria today, Franz! First you have to dress a gentleman up as a lady. Then you have to dress a bankrupt corsetmaker's son up as a gentleman. Herr Goldmann, from the Vienna slums, now acting the part of Herr Reinhardt, proprietor of a baroque palace. Luziwuzi may have been a lady, but at least he was a gentleman.

**Franz**   Sir.

**Müller**   And now Herr Goldmann is offering us a play addressing the problem of excessive wealth. I hadn't realised that it was quite so pressing. We've just lost the Great War. The currency has collapsed. So we have various problems. Unemployment. Hunger. Disease. People seeing their entire life savings wiped out. But *wealth*? Do you feel that wealth is putting *your* immortal soul in jeopardy?

**Franz**   Not in my place to say, sir.

**Müller**   'Not in my place to say, sir.' Forty rooms! When people are living on the streets! So, he's descended from the metropolitan heights of Berlin to come and save our souls in poor little provincial Salzburg. Or was he on the way down in the world anyway? Going out of fashion with the critics and the public in Berlin? And did he pick Salzburg because of our particular spiritual need? Or because there happened to be a baroque palace here that my desperate fellow-countrymen were selling for next to nothing? 'Not in my place to say, sir.'

*Enter* **Kommer**.

**Müller**   But perhaps the day will come when it will be. When we all pluck up our courage and say what we think about such things.

**Kommer** (*to* **Müller**)   You're still with us? What are you *doing* here?

**Müller**   The same as the rest of you. Drinking Herr Goldmann's champagne. Eating his *foie gras*.

**Kommer**   And who invited you?

**Müller**   I did.

**Kommer**   Franz, show this gentleman out. The odd coin –
yes. But not champagne and *foie gras*.

**Franz**   This way, if you please, sir.

**Müller** (*takes the plate of canapés*)   The children in town might
like something to eat . . .

*Exit* **Müller**. *Enter* **Reinhardt, Prince Archbishop, Thimig,**
*and* **Adler**.

**Reinhardt**   God created the world. But man, whom He
created in His image, has created a second world in His turn.
The world of art.

**Prince Archbishop**   This house.

**Reinhardt**   Certain ways of living.

**Prince Archbishop**   Your play.

**Reinhardt**   Indeed, our play.

**Prince Archbishop**   A banquet has been ordained, has it
not? Guests are expected. But Death is on his way! How will
Death respond when he finds Everyman living in such style?
Will he allow himself to be seduced? Will he forget the summons
he is bearing? We are all in suspense.

**Reinhardt**
    Day's toil is done. Soft darkness falls.
    Sweet sounds of music fill my halls.

*Lights down. Music.*

**Adler** (*reads*)   Enter Guests with lanterns.

*Enter* **Thomas, Josef, Liesl,** *and* **Gretl** *with lanterns. Party noise.*

**Adler**   A table appears, richly laid and set with lights.

*A table appears, richly laid and set with lights.*

Enter Everyman's Mistress.

*She looks at* **Thimig**, *who glances at* **Reinhardt** *and hesitates. He*
*nods.*

**Thimig**

Thy guests all wait impatiently
Their good and gen'rous host to see.
To fetch him thither am I come
With pipe and timbrel, shawm and drum.

**Reinhardt**

Oh, mistress mine! At once I feel
The hot blood through my body steal!

**Adler** (*reads*)   She kisses him –

**Thimig** *kisses* **Reinhardt**.

**Adler** (*reads*)   – And sets a wreath of brightly coloured flowers
on his head.

**Thimig** *produces a rose and fixes it in* **Reinhardt***'s buttonhole.*

**Reinhardt**

Thy beauty doth the lamps outshine,
Thy voice is sweeter than sweet wine –
A balsam to my weary heart
That easeth every ache and smart.

(*To everyone.*)

New love, old friends – what more need we
To make all care and sorrow flee?
A glass of wine, a snatch of song –
Can mortal man for aught else long?
Most dear you are to me, my friends!
Enjoy the pleasures that life sends!
So raise the cup! Drink deep, drink long!
Lift up the voice! Sing sweet, sing strong!

**Thomas**, **Josef**, **Liesl**, **Gretl** (*sing in harmony*)

Oh, here's to you, our merry host,
May all your troubles fly!
To you we drink this cheerful toast –
Live, live until you die!

God send you luck, God send you wealth,
And praises to the sky!

God send you love, God send you health –
Live, live until you die!

**All** ( *join in*)
As long as life and breath shall last
We'll sing it low and high!
We'll sing it slow, we'll sing it fast –
Live, live until you die!

**Death** (*off, huge and terrible, from different quarters, drowning the song, but heard only by* **Reinhardt**)
Everyman! Everyman!

**Reinhardt**
Who called?

*The singing dies away.*

My name! Who called my name?
A voice that from the darkness came,
And through my heart like quickfire ran.
Who rudely so called 'Everyman'?

**Thimig**
'Twas but the echo of our song
That in thy hearing lingered on.

**Reinhardt**
No, no – the voice that I heard call
Came not with soft and dying fall
But like high thunder through the land.
So: 'Everyman!' And 'Everyman!'
I knew that voice! Yet knew it not!
Or knew it once, and had forgot!
A voice that echoed down the years,
And now will ever haunt my ears.
From nowhere, everywhere it came . . .

**Death** (*off, whispers*)
Everyman! Everyman!

**Reinhardt**
And comes again, and comes again!

**Death**

> Everyman! Everyman!

**Thimig**

> No voice hear I, nor any sound.
> All silent stand thy guests around.
> Thy cheek is pale, thy hand is chill –
> Thou hast mayhap some sudden ill.

*The darkness deepens.*

**Reinhardt**

> Now darker grows the gath'ring night . . .
> Unsure the candles' flickering light . . .

*The masked and cloaked figure of* **Death** *becomes visible in the shadows.*

**Reinhardt**

> Methinks I see a strange face there
> With eyes that coldly at me stare!

**Death** *steps forward, and becomes visible to the others. They utter a gasp or horror and freeze.*

**Death**

> In merry mood do I thee find.
> Of Him who made thee hast thou mind?

**Reinhardt**

> Why come'st thou here to question me?
> What have these things to do with thee?

**Death**

> On God's high mission am I bent.
> To seek thee out He hath me sent
> And fetch thee thence with urgent speed.

**Reinhardt**

> How so? Of me what hath He need?

**Death**

> While yet of Him thou thinkest not,
> He hath not thee likewise forgot.

**Reinhardt**

Of me in what wise thinketh He?

**Death**

That soon and plainly shalt thou see.
To thee He bade me straightly say:
A reckoning will He have! Today!

**Reinhardt**

And who art thou, who art so bold
The Almighty's purpose to unfold?

**Death**

My name is Death. I favour none,
Nor any fear. To all I come.

*The others shrink away from him.*

Quick now, make haste, no more delay!
A long road must thou walk today.
Thou trav'lest to that far-off land
Where thou before God's throne shalt stand,
And there, for thy day's work, shalt draw
Thy wages – neither less nor more.
What – hast thou like a fool believed
That this thy life, from God received,
And these thy earthly goods, were *thine*?

**Reinhardt**

I did believe that they were mine.

**Death**

Not so. They were but held in trust.
Inherit them another must.
Until on him I shall attend –
And his lease, too, be at an end.

**Reinhardt**

Yet grant me, I do thee implore,
One day on earth, one short day, more!
I fain would seek some company
To walk this fearful road with me,
That when I stand before God's throne
I stand not nakedly alone.

*Pause.*

**Death**

Thy prayer I grant. Go! One more day!
Make thou wise use of this brief stay!

**Death** *vanishes. Lights up. Everyone laughs and relaxes.*

**Reinhardt**

So Death gives Everyman a space,
To mend and then present his case.
Grant us the same, Your Grace – a day
To mend and then present our play.

**Prince Archbishop**

No less than Death himself am I
A servant of great God on high.
How can it then be meet for me
To be less generous than He?
Besides, I'm all on fire to know
How things for Everyman will go.
So childish of me! Even worse,
I do believe I'm speaking verse.

*The* **Prince Archbishop** *blesses them and exits.*

**Thimig**

You saw? He raised his hand to bless!

**Reinhardt**

I think that means . . .

**Kommer**

. . . the answer's yes!

*Cheers. Raised glasses.*

But . . . who played Death, then? Death was who?

**Thomas**

Not me.

**Kommer**

So you?

**Josef**

           Nor me.

**Kommer** (*to* **Franz**)

                Nor you?

**Reinhardt**
  Some stranger, doing good by stealth!

*Exit all except* **Franz**.

**Franz**   I saw his eyes. 'Twas Death himself.

*Darkness.*

**Thomas** (*as Prologue*)
  Draw near, good people all, I pray!
  Give heed while we perform our play –

*Daylight. On a lower level downstage* **Thomas** *is rehearsing. Above him, upstage,* **Reinhardt**, *immaculate as ever, watches, with* **Adler**, **Liesl** *and* **Gretl**, *who quietly set a rehearsal table and supply him with pencils, coffee, the prompt-book, etc.*

**Thomas**
  – Wherein we show, as best we can,
  The Summoning of Everyman.
  Here all shall learn, with eyes to see,
  How short our days on earth do be,
  How sorrowful must be our end,
  Should we our ways neglect to mend . . .

**Reinhardt**   Thank you. From the beginning again, please. 'Draw near, good people all, I pray . . . '

**Thomas**
  Draw near, good people all, I pray . . .

**Reinhardt** (*demonstrates*)
  Draw near, good people all, I pray . . .

**Thomas** (*attempts to imitate*)
  Draw near, good people all, I pray . . .

**Reinhardt**
  Draw near, good people all, I pray . . .

**Thomas**

 Draw near, good people all, I pray . . .

**Reinhardt** (*always calm, collected, and patient*)   What we are
trying to achieve is very simple. It is perfection. Simple
perfection. Life is not perfect. It is confused and elusive and
shabby. We have six weeks in which to make one small piece
of it, approximately four hundred metres square by two hours
long, into something that we can lay before our benefactor,
the Prince Archbishop of Salzburg, and all the other citizens
of this town. Something of which we can say, Look, this is how
life really is!

*He picks up the prompt-book and demonstrates it.*

This is life, this is death, when all the confusion and shabbiness
have been stripped away, when we really look at them and get
hold of them. They are part of each other. Everything is
inextricably part of everything. And yet, for these two short
hours, it is also very simple and very elegant. That is what we
are trying to achieve together. Yes? Once again, then, if you
please . . .

**Adler**   Herr Reinhardt . . .

**Reinhardt**

 Draw near, good people all, I pray . . . !

**Adler**   I'm sorry. You wanted me to remind you about your
cable to New York . . .

**Reinhardt**   Draft something for me, will you, Gusti?

**Adler**   And your mother's birthday. I'll get another silk
scarf . . . Oh, and there is a problem with the whores. For the
banquet scene this afternoon. We will only have six whores.

**Reinhardt**   Six? I asked for twenty.

*Hammering.*

**Adler**   Would you hold the hammering . . . ? *Hammering . . . !*
Thank you . . . Two of them are off sick, Herr Reinhardt. One's
got choir practice. One's taking her school-leaving exam . . .

**Reinhardt**    That still leaves sixteen.

**Adler**    No, because Katie said . . .

**Reinhardt**    *Katie* said?

*Enter* **Kommer**.

**Kommer**    Ten. Katie said ten whores.

**Reinhardt** (*patiently*)    I want twenty.

**Kommer**    You won't have noticed this, but we have a production budget.

**Reinhardt**    Twenty whores.

**Kommer**    We have exceeded the production budget. The production is in deficit. There is also a world economic crisis. The country is going smash.

*Hammering.*

Will you stop that noise . . . ! (*To* **Reinhardt**.) We have no money to pay any more whores. We have no costumes for any more whores. There are no more whores in Salzburg.

**Reinhardt**    I want twenty whores.

**Kommer**    You want two hundred whores! But you can't have them!

**Reinhardt**    I don't want two hundred whores. I am trying to purge the theatre of excess. I am trying to produce this play in the simplest imaginable way with the simplest imaginable means. But it is physically impossible to stage this particular scene with less than twenty whores.

**Adler**    When Herr Reinhardt was doing *The Miracle* in Vienna . . .

**Kommer**    He had a thousand extras.

**Adler**    He had fifteen hundred extras.

**Kommer**    And everyone thought it was completely ridiculous! The notices were terrible! There were more extras than audience!

**Adler**   Excuse me – there were nine thousand in the audience.

**Reinhardt**   My brother made no difficulties about finding me fifteen hundred extras.

**Kommer**   Your brother, your brother!

**Reinhardt**   Be careful what you say about my brother, please.

**Kommer**   Your other self – I know, I know! The only soul in the world you actually love. And he understands money. Which you don't. And I don't, and no one does, only your beloved brother. So ask *him* for whores!

**Adler**   His brother has more important things to think about than a few extras! He has Herr Reinhardt's entire business empire to manage! He has two huge theatres to run!

**Reinhardt**   So, more whores by this afternoon.

**Kommer**   By this afternoon you will have my resignation in your hands.

**Adler**   We still have it from last week.

**Kommer**   Excellent. Then I can leave at once.

**Reinhardt**   The whores first, though, please. Now if we can possibly get on with the rehearsal . . .

*Enter* **Franz** *with documents.*

**Reinhardt**   Bills? Anything to do with money – give it to Katie.

**Kommer**   No money. No Katie.

**Franz** (*to* **Reinhardt**)   It's the dwarfs, Herr Reinhardt.

**Reinhardt**   Dwarfs?

**Franz**   Two of them have come without their heads. For the garden, Herr Reinhardt.

**Reinhardt**   Katie will deal with it.

**Kommer**   Katie *won't* deal with it. Katie has resigned.

**Reinhardt**   From the beginning of the scene, please.

Draw near, good people all, I pray . . .

Death . . . Where is Death?

**Adler**   He had a costume-fitting this morning, Herr Reinhardt. Shall I run and see how long he's going to be?

**Reinhardt**   Katie can do it on his way to deal with the dwarfs. Katie!

**Kommer**   He never takes the slightest notice of anything I say! I resign, and he doesn't even hear it!

*He begins to leave.*

Also it's going to pour with rain. You want me to get the rain stopped?

**Reinhardt**   If you would be so kind. And, Katie . . . more whores!

*Exit* **Kommer** *and* **Franz**. **Reinhardt** *waits patiently. Enter* **Thimig**.

**Thimig**   Time, Gusti! Time, time, time! He never has enough time! Every night he sits up half the night rewriting that prompt-book . . . What time did you get to bed last night, Reinhardt?

**Reinhardt**   Last night? I had an early night for once.

**Thimig** (*to* **Adler**)   An early night. That's two or three o'clock. Then of course he's exhausted, and he gets up late. But he will never hurry! Twenty minutes every morning to clean his teeth!

*Enter* **Franz** *holding a selection of ties.*

**Thimig**   Then it's the suit . . . And the tie . . .

**Adler**   He wants everything to be just right, Helene! The play. The house. His appearance.

**Franz**   Or perhaps the blue, Herr Reinhardt.

**Reinhardt** (*examines himself in the looking glass*)   Perhaps the blue . . .

*He unhurriedly takes off the tie he is wearing and tries* **Franz**'s *selection.*

**Thimig**   Reinhardt! You will be late for rehearsal! You're always late for rehearsal! You keep everyone waiting!

**Reinhardt**   I *am* rehearsing, Leni. I am rehearsing myself.

**Thimig**   Always late! Always exhausted! Never any time!

**Adler**   He doesn't want to have any time left over, does he, Helene, with nothing to fill it? Nothing in front of him. Nothing in his head. Nothing to do.

**Reinhardt**   I think the blue is a little adventurous.

*He unhurriedly changes back to his original tie.*

**Adler**   And don't worry, Helene. He always gets everything done. It's all down here in the diary . . . Auditions at eleven, Herr Reinhardt. Costume-designer at twelve . . . And the rehearsal schedule, Herr Reinhardt. Prologue . . .

*Enter* **Thomas**, *as Prologue.*

**Thomas**
   Draw near, good people all, I pray . . .

*Continues the speech in the background, repeating if necessary.*

**Adler**   House . . .

*Enter* **Josef**, *as Everyman.*

**Josef**
   A lordly house I own and fair . . .

*Continues likewise.*

**Adler**   Poor Neighbour . . .

*Enter* **Franz**.

**Franz**
   I dwelt once in a house as fine . . .

*Continues likewise.*

**Adler**    Banquet . . .

*Enter* **Liesl**.

**Liesl**
Thy guests all wait impatiently . . .

*Continues likewise.*

**Adler**    Prologue again . . .

**Thomas**
Draw near, good people all, I pray . . .

*Continues likewise.*

**Reinhardt** *finishes tying his tie, and raises his hand for silence. The overlaid voices die away.*

**Reinhardt**    And there we are. Once again. Ready to face the world. Ready to go before the judgment seat.

**Adler**    Beginners, please . . . ! Quiet, everyone . . . Quiet backstage . . . !

*Everyone scatters. The expectant murmur of an audience.*

**Reinhardt**    Listen, listen!

**Adler**    An audience!

**Thimig**    The sound they make! That terrifying sound!

**Reinhardt**    I know what Everyman felt as he took his stand in the courtroom. Already dead. And intensely conscious of being alive. Why do we do it, Leni? Why do we put ourselves through it?

**Adler**    Toi toi toi, Herr Reinhardt! Toi toi toi, Helene!

**Kommer**, **Müller**, *the* **Prince Archbishop**, **Josef**, **Thomas**, **Gretl**, *and* **Liesl** *appear in various places, looking out into the auditorium, together with* **Franz**, *waiting.*

**Reinhardt**    Full house?

**Kommer**   Full square.

**Adler**   Two minutes, everyone . . . !

**Reinhardt**   Who have we got out there?

**Kommer**   Everyman, by the look of it.

**Müller**   Every man in Salzburg who can afford the luxury of being told by Herr Goldmann that he shouldn't have.

**Reinhardt**   Yap, yap! What *is* it that they all find to talk about . . . ?

**Kommer**   It's going to rain, it's going to rain, it's going to rain . . .

**Franz**   What happens when they all open their umbrellas . . . ?

**Adler**   One minute . . . Good luck, everyone . . .

*Thimig blows* **Reinhardt** *a kiss.* **Kommer** *bobs his head, praying.* **Reinhardt** *looks at him. He stops.* **Adler** *puts down the diary and takes up the prompt-book. She watches* **Reinhardt***, waiting for the order to start. He nods. She signals to someone off.*

**Adler**   Cue music . . . Cue cathedral doors . . . Cue cast . . .

*The offstage audience quietens.*

**Thomas** (*as Prologue, off, distant, echoing round the square*)
    Draw near, good people all, I pray!
    Give heed while we perform our play,
    Wherein we show, as best we can,
    The Summoning of Everyman . . .

*Everyone finds a place to sit. The faint echoing murmur of voices from the stage continues off.*

**Adler**   Cue God . . . Cue Everyman . . .

**Reinhardt** (*to himself*)   Settle down! Don't rush it! Wait for them to come to you . . .

**Adler**   Cue Poor Neighbour . . . Cue Mistress . . . Cue Banquet . . .

*Faint sounds of music and party noise.*

Cue Death . . .

**Death** (*off*)    Everyman! Everyman! Everyman!

*The noise and music suddenly die away.* **Reinhardt** *stands.*

**Josef** (*as Everyman, off*)
    Who called?

**Reinhardt**, *intent, absently begins to mouth the words of the offstage speech.*

**Josef** (*as Everyman, off*)
    My name! Who called my name?
    A voice that from the darkness came,
    And through my heart like quickfire ran.
    Who rudely so called 'Everyman' . . . ?

**Thimig**    Words, words. Words and weather.

**Adler**    Chill flurries of wind off the mountains.

*The light begins to fade. Only* **Adler**, **Reinhardt** *and* **Thimig** *remain lit.*

**Thimig**    The shadows in the square gradually lengthening.

**Adler**    The summer twilight creeping in.

**Thimig**    Night falling . . .

**Reinhardt** *mouths Everyman's words along with* **Josef.**

**Josef** (*off*)
    Eternal God! Eternal light!
    Eternal way of truth and right!
    In my last moment, as I die,
    Hear Thou my cry, Lord, hear my cry!

    Now down into the grave I go,
    Down, down into the dark below.

**Thimig** *mouths Faith's words along with* **Liesl.**

**Liesl** (*off*)
    Thy Faith by thee will faithful stand.

**Adler** *does the same with Works's words along with* **Gretl**.

**Gretl** (*off*)
> And I, thy Works, at thy right hand.

**Liesl** (*off*)
> I hear the angels' heavenly song.
> Their voices ring out sweet and strong
> Poor weary souls to welcome in.
> For him it is, methinks, they sing.

*The angels sing. Music. The last light on* **Reinhardt** *fades to darkness. Applause, off.*

*Lights up.* **Reinhardt**, **Thimig**, **Adler**, **Kommer**, *and* **Franz** *listen to the applause, trying to judge it.*

**Reinhardt**    Yes? No? Yes . . . ?

**Kommer**    Possibly.

**Reinhardt**    And His Grace?

**Adler** *indicates him. He is still sitting, forgotten, dabbing a handkerchief to his eyes.*

**Thimig**    Your Grace . . . ?

**Prince Archbishop** (*smiles through his tears*)    Happy ending!

*They are all relieved. Laughter. Embraces.*

**Adler**    Now all we have to do is . . .

**Thimig**    Do it again!

**Adler**    And again!

**Thimig**    And again!

**Prince Archbishop**    But, my son, my son, one day he will come for *you*, that fearful messenger!

**Reinhardt**    He will come for all of us, Your Grace.

**Prince Archbishop**    For all of us, for all of us. But, my dear boy – *you* will not hear the angels sing! You will go down into the pit, and you will be gone for all eternity! You don't

understand the images you have conjured up . . . And yet
something in you longs to. Isn't that why you have produced
this play?

**Kommer**    Never mind that.

> Herr Reinhardt says, it being a first night,
> He doth everyone back to his house invite.
> His cooks have a light supper conjured up
> On which His Grace and other dignitaries might care to sup!

*Exit all noisily, except* **Thimig**. *Sudden quiet.*

**Thimig**    Listen!

*Enter* **Adler**, *holding mail.*

**Adler**    What? What . . . ?

**Thimig**    Nothing! Silence. Everything – vanished like a
dream!

**Adler**    The season's over. They've broken up the stage.

**Thimig**    Just you and me, creeping about an empty house.

**Adler**    The leaves are falling.

**Thimig**    Autumn . . . Winter . . .

**Adler**    Snow on the mountains . . . Snow hiding the garden . . .

**Thimig**    The house is full of pale light. Great empty staring
rooms where nothing ever happens. Where's it all gone, Gusti?
All the rush, all the long days and late nights? All the exhaustion?

**Adler**    It's moving around the world with Reinhardt.

*She lays out mail.* **Thimig** *picks it up.*

**Thimig**    Vienna, Berlin . . . Paris, London . . . New York,
Los Angeles . . .

**Adler**    Plays . . . operas . . . All over the world they want
him, Helene! You never see him!

**Thimig**    Every day he writes. Telegrams, letters. (*Reads.*)
'Disaster . . . ' 'Triumph . . . ' 'Encouraged . . . ' 'Exhausted . . . '

**Adler**   'Call Richard Strauss commission new opera . . . '

**Thimig**   'Call Bernard Shaw commission play life Christ . . . '

**Adler**   He's worrying about the house. 'Contract for work on roof . . . ' 'Quotations for rewiring . . . '

**Thimig**   And the garden. 'Twenty-one mature orange trees . . . '

**Adler**   'Herons for the lake . . . ' 'Sea-horses for the terrace . . . '

**Thimig**   Then suddenly it's summer again. And once again, on the Cathedral Square . . .

*Enter* **Reinhardt**.

**Reinhardt**
Draw near, good people all, I pray!
Give heed while we perform our play . . .

**Thimig**   *Everyman*! Again!

**Adler**   Rehearsals, rehearsals.

**Thimig**   First night.

**Adler**   And again they listen. Again the Prince Archbishop weeps.

**Thimig**   Why do they want to know about death, Gusti?

**Adler**   And already it's the last night.

**Thimig**   Over. Dead and gone. Like Everyman himself. And Reinhardt is on the road again.

**Adler**   Cables from New York . . . Telegrams from Berlin . . . Winter. Summer . . .

**Reinhardt**
Draw near, good people all, I pray . . . !

**Adler**   Then next year.

**Reinhardt**
Draw near, good people all . . . !

**Thimig**    Then every year.

**Reinhardt**
  Draw near, good people . . . !

**Adler**    Each autumn it vanishes, like the summer itself, as if
it had never been.

**Thimig**    And each summer, like summer, it returns.

**Adler**    (*fetches the prompt-book*)    House . . . Banquet . . . Money . . .
Money scene, please! Money scene!

*Enter* **Josef**, *as Everyman, and* **Thomas**, **Liesl**, *and* **Gretl** *with
rehearsal table and boxes of props.*

**Reinhardt**    Everyman!

  My money hath much work to do . . .

**Josef**
  My money hath much work to do –
  Must dig and sow and build and hew . . .

**Reinhardt**    Simply, simply! A man telling us as innocently as
a child about the problems of good fortune. No irony! No hint
of what's to come . . . !

  My money hath much work to do –
  Must dig and sow and build and hew,
  Nor ever pause nor ever sleep,
  If I my just reward will reap . . .

**Josef**, **Thomas**, **Liesl**, *and* **Gretl** *carry in Old Masters, antique
furniture, statues, etc.*

  Yes, great may be my wealth – but great
  The cost of running my estate.
  My servants must have coats and bread,
  My dogs and horses must be fed,
  My parks and pleasure gardens made,
  My gamekeepers and bailiffs paid.
  My hunting grounds must be secured,
  My private fishing rights ensured.
  And constantly must things be mended,

Renewed, replaced, improved, extended.
The more one hath, the more immense
Becomes the burden of expense . . .

*Enter* **Kommer**, *holding documents.*

**Kommer**
The more one hath, the more one fills
Th' entire house with unpaid bills!

And tax. More tax. You already owe so much back tax that it's being discussed by the government at ministerial level.

**Reinhardt**   Money, money! I have other things to think about!

**Kommer**   What I can never decide, Herr Reinhardt, is whether you are feeble-minded, or whether you are an imposter. Everyone in the world is one or the other! Professionally you are an imposter, and I honour you for it, because you are able to put on a performance that convinces actors, audiences, and archbishops alike. But when it comes to money . . .

**Reinhardt**   When it comes to money – I leave all that to my brother.

**Kommer**   Your brother, thank God, is an imposter through and through, like me, and without him your great empire would collapse like a rotten mushroom. But where is even your brother going to find the kind of money you now owe?

**Adler**   He can raise another loan!

**Kommer**   Another loan? Excellent idea! On the security of what?

**Adler**   Of this house! He's done it before!

**Kommer**   He certainly has. We have six mortgages on the security of this house. Not to mention the furniture. Or the pictures and statues. This house, which is supporting the weight of not only enough artwork and statuary to satisfy Lorenzo the Magnificent but also the greater part of all serious theatre in German-speaking Europe, is entirely constructed out of debt.

It is a monument not so much of baroque architecture as of baroque pawnbroking.

*Enter* **Thimig**, *holding a telegram.*

**Kommer**    And, if I may quote from the wisdom of Everyman in the play:

> It followeth, as B from A,
> And always hath, since Adam's day:
> Who buildeth house, and needs must borrow,
> Will build a house of pain and sorrow . . .

(*To* **Thimig**.) Not another bill?

**Adler**    A telegram . . . ? Helene! What is it?

**Thimig** (*to* **Reinhardt**)    I'm so sorry . . .

*She hands him the telegram.*

You loved him. We all loved him.

**Reinhardt** *reads the telegram.*

**Death** (*off, distant*)    Everyman! Everyman!

**Adler**    His brother?

**Reinhardt** *goes out.*

**Adler**    Oh, no! Oh, Helene! Whatever are we going to do without him?

**Thimig**    What everyone always does. Miss him. And wonder how we'll ever manage. And manage. And remember him. And then forget him.

*Exit* **Thimig** *after* **Reinhardt**.

**Adler**    Poor Edmund!

**Kommer**    Poor us.

**Adler**    Katie! We can't think about the money now!

**Kommer**    Someone will have to. Another imposter.

*Enter* **Reinhardt**.

**Kommer**   And who is the only other real imposter we know . . . ?

*Exit* **Kommer**.

**Reinhardt**   And on we go.

Draw near, good people all, I pray . . . !

**Adler** *settles to the prompt-book.*

**Adler**   Which scenes are we doing, Herr Reinhardt?

**Reinhardt**   The same as last year and the year before. The same as next year and the year after. Prologue, Banquet, Death . . . House, Money . . . Money, Money . . .

My money hath much work to do –
Must dig and sow and build and hew . . .

Poor Neighbour:

No mortal ill can do worse harm
Than money, with its cursed charm . . .

*Enter* **Kommer**. *He silently holds out a document and a pen to* **Reinhardt**.

**Reinhardt**
In glitt'ring spiderwebs of gold
Doth Satan seek us to enfold.
Whoso succumbeth to that spell
Embarketh on the path to hell.

*He takes the document and pen as he continues.*

Everyman . . .

Thou fool, this benison to despise!
Learn this from me: the man was wise
Who first the great discov'ry made . . .

(*To* **Kommer**.) Something to do with money?

**Kommer**   I read, you sign.

**Reinhardt** (*signs as he speaks*)
> The man was wise
> Who first the great discov'ry made,
> And elevated thus our trade
> From petty barter and exchange
> To nobler aims and wider range.

*He hands the document back but keeps the pen.* **Kommer** *waits, hand out.*

**Reinhardt**
> Once money shows her smiling face
> Our world becomes a better place,
> For each man in his chosen field
> A godlike power doth learn to wield.

*He pats his pockets as he speaks.*

> He can command the seeds to grow
> And make the living waters flow,
> Send this man here and that man there,
> Make square the round and round the square,
> For naught there is on low or high
> That money cannot sell or buy.

*He finds a handful of banknotes.*

> Admire this rare and wond'rous thing!
> That serves as slave and rules as king,
> That answers every beck and call,
> Yet holds all men within its thrall!

*He hands the banknotes to* **Kommer**, *who looks at them.*

**Reinhardt**    What?

**Kommer**    This? It appears to be *money*. You appear to be giving me *money*. Is this a *tip*?

**Reinhardt**    I'm sorry. You had your hand out.

*He takes them back.* **Kommer** *takes them off him again.*

**Kommer**    You're not carrying cash around? You're not giving tips?

**Reinhardt**    I am trying to take control of my financial affairs.

**Kommer**    Of about four times the average monthly wage?

**Reinhardt**    But I cannot count out money and direct at the same time.

**Kommer**    *I* look after the money! *Franz* looks after the money! *I* hand out the tips! *Franz* hands out the tips! Fräulein Thimig, Fräulein Adler – the second under-gardener and the third under-footman – anyone. But not you, if you please, Herr Reinhardt!

**Reinhardt**    I accept that I don't understand money . . .

**Kommer**    'I don't understand money!' Do you think *I* understand money? Do you think *Rothschild* understands money? *Nobody* understands money!

**Reinhardt**    My brother actually did understand money.

**Kommer**    What your sainted brother understood, God rest him, was how to pay the lowest wages in Europe. And persuade people to accept them because it was such an honour to work for you. What he understood was how to make you hear what he said when he said no. Of me you take no notice whatsoever, and we are all going smash! The house, the city, the festival! The whole country! So, my revered Herr Reinhardt, any waiters with their hands out, any beggars, anyone collecting for charity – refer them to me. I know I can never replace your brother. But somehow I have got myself in the position where I *am* replacing your brother! So I have to *act the part* of a man who understands money! *Someone* has to, otherwise nothing would happen! No house, no cathedral to perform your simple morality play in front of! No simple morality play! No simplicity! No morality!

**Reinhardt** *retreats.* **Kommer** *pursues him.*

**Kommer**    'Admire this rare and wond'rous thing!' Yes? And since I have many columns of figures to add up and balance out, perhaps you would be kind enough to return my *pen* . . . ?

*Exit* **Reinhardt** *and* **Kommer**. *Enter* **Thimig**, *holding telegrams and letters.*

**Thimig**    Autumn again . . . Winter . . . It's always autumn! It's always winter! He's nothing but letters and telegrams!

**Adler**    'Cable producers Philadephia . . . ' 'Check bookings Rome . . . '

**Thimig**    'Cast contracts *Everyman* . . . ' 'Three hundred rose-bushes . . . ' It's never even autumn, it's never even winter! It's not *now*! It's never *now*! It's always next season!

**Adler**    Next season on tour.

**Thimig**    Next season in the garden.

**Adler**    Next season in Salzburg.

**Thimig**    And then suddenly . . .

**Adler**    The snow has gone from the mountains.

**Thimig**    The garden is green.

**Adler**    Next season is this season.

**Thimig**    Now is now.

*Enter* **Reinhardt**. *He and* **Thimig** *look at each other, smiling.*

**Adler**    Oh, Herr Reinhardt! Welcome home! Did you have a good crossing, Herr Reinhardt? Was New York impossible? The advance on *Everyman* is twelve per cent up on last year. Oh, and the new altarpiece has arrived. And Graz is up in arms because they say you're going to do the Pirandello in Linz first, and New York must have the final dates for the tour of the *Dream*. Also one of the monkeys has bitten the kitchenmaid, and the new flamingos are not the same pink as the old ones. Also . . .

**Thimig**    Gusti! Go and help Franz unpack!

**Adler**    Oh . . . yes, of course. I'm sorry, Helene. I'm sorry, Herr Reinhardt.

*Exit* **Adler**.

**Reinhardt**   My wonderful house! The only production of mine that will endure. Everything else is written on the wind.

**Thimig**   The house . . . and the garden . . .

**Reinhardt**
> Let me, I pray thee, take thy hand
> And lead thee into thine own land.
> For thy delight, my fairest fair,
> Do I this pleasure park prepare –
> Our Eden, where we may enjoy
> The happy hours without annoy.
> Here nature doth conspire with art
> To please the eye and glad the heart.
> In this dear place thou mayest see
> A token of my love for thee.

**Thimig**
> Here hast thou planted many a flower
> To deck with jewels each golden hour!
> The lily here – and here the rose –
> And here sweet honeysuckle grows
> To freight with heavy-swooning musk
> The dewy morn, the lang'rous dusk.
> Here woodland walks and many a glade
> Extend a soft and verdant shade
> Whereto we haply may retreat
> To scape the drowsy noonday heat,
> And by cool springs and winding streams
> Long wander lost in summer dreams.

**Reinhardt**
> If thou find'st here, in this green place,
> Some cloudy mirror for thy grace,
> Some passing moment of delight,
> It will thy gard'ner's pains requite.

*Peace, quiet.* **Reinhardt** *sits and closes his eyes. Enter* **Adler**.

**Adler**   I'm sorry, Herr Reinhardt. I'm sorry, Helene . . .

**Thimig**   Gusti, I am trying to give Reinhardt a few precious moments of peace!

**Adler**  Yes, but his wife has telephoned.

**Thimig**  Oh, *no*! Reinhardt! (*To* **Reinhardt**.) I thought you
had told her *not* to telephone? I thought she had *promised*!
What did she want?

**Adler**  She wanted to talk to Herr Reinhardt.

**Thimig**  Of course! Reinhardt, don't pretend you're asleep.
That woman is poisoning our lives! I have tried to make our
home a refuge for you. But how can I, when she keeps pursuing
us? You and I both want to live quietly and peacefully together
like any other couple. But we can't until we've got you divorced!
I know how difficult that is. It's the same as with this house. Or
the play. Making something simple and natural is very complex.
I know you can't get a divorce in Austria . . .

**Adler**  Or anywhere else. She won't give him one! His
brother tried and tried to find a way round it! But not even *he*
could do it!

**Thimig**  Maybe because his brother could read his mind,
and he knew he doesn't really want one.

**Adler**  Doesn't really want one? Helene, what do you mean?
Of course he wants one! He's been all over Europe trying to
get one!

**Thimig**  The present arrangement is rather convenient for
him, isn't it? Isn't it, Reinhardt? It means you don't have to
marry *me*! I'm just part of the house! I'm just one of the
artworks!

**Adler**  Helene! I really don't think that is quite fair to Herr
Reinhardt. He loves you. He wants to marry you.

**Thimig**  Gusti, the fact that you and I were at school
together doesn't give you the right to tell me whether people
love me and want to marry me! That's not why I asked you to
come and work for Herr Reinhardt!

**Adler**  You asked me to come and work for him because you
wanted to make his life a little easier.

**Reinhardt**  Ladies . . .

**Adler**   And also, no doubt, because you thought that whoever he runs off with next at least it won't be *me*!

**Thimig**   Gusti, control yourself! I know you worship the ground he walks upon. There's nothing very special about that, Gusti! *Everyone* worships the ground he walks upon! Even Katie! Even his wife! But you make a fool of him, Gusti! You don't stand up to him! You always let him have his way! And how can we ever discuss anything between us if you immediately take his side?

**Adler**   Helene!

**Thimig**   His wife telephones – you take *her* side!

**Adler**   You know that's not true!

**Thimig**   I can't think why Reinhardt *needs* a personal assistant. Everything you do for him I could perfectly well do myself.

**Adler**   You have your own work to do! You're an actress, not a secretary! You're away in Vienna, you're off on tour!

**Thimig**   And if it's like this when I'm here, heaven knows what it's like when I'm not!

*Pause.*

**Reinhardt**   Do you think we should try to find another figure to go at the end of the avenue there? Something very still and very calm?

**Thimig**   I'm sorry to get upset. But this is our home. We made it together. When we have guests, when the Prince Archbishop comes, I want to stand in the great hall and receive him, like any other wife in the world. I want to say goodbye to him at the end of the evening.

**Adler**   Helene, you *do* say goodbye to him at the end of the evening!

**Thimig**   As *I* leave! I want to say goodbye to him as *he* leaves!

**Adler**   Our relations with the local citizens are bad enough as it is.

**Thimig**   Anyway, Katie says you can get one in Latvia.

**Adler**   A divorce? In Latvia?

**Thimig**   It's just a matter of six months' residence.

**Adler**   He has to go to Paris, Helene. Then Stockholm. Then he's got the American tour.

**Thimig**   After the American tour.

**Adler**   He has to take his sons on holiday.

**Thimig**   His sons can come here.

**Adler**   Helene, if the boys come here *she* has to come, too! She has a court order!

**Thimig**   And there you go, taking his side again! Why don't you invite his *daughter's* mother as well? And that female drug fiend who always descends as soon as my back is turned? And that other trollop in London? – Yes, I *do* know about her!

*Enter* **Kommer**.

**Thimig**   And Katie! You can all fight over him together . . . !

**Kommer**   I hate to interrupt this idyll . . .

*He shows documents.*

**Adler**   *Another* tax demand?

**Kommer**   A German one this time.

**Reinhardt**   Money. I am to leave all questions of money to you, I believe.

*Exit* **Reinhardt**.

**Adler** (*reads the tax demand*)   Oh, my God!

**Kommer**   Exactly. Herr Hitler is obviously taking a personal interest in ruining him.

**Thimig**   What do you want him to do about it? Chop down the trees and build holiday homes? Go off on tour again? He's only just come back! You will kill that man!

*Enter* **Reinhardt**.

**Reinhardt**   And Gusti – the zoo place in Hamburg. We need a few pelicans. About a dozen. Also nightingales. Chinese nightingales.

*Exit* **Reinhardt**.

**Thimig**   Reinhardt! Wait! The new altarpiece! We must get another altar to put it over . . . !

*Exit* **Thimig**.

**Adler**   So what are you suggesting?

**Kommer**   This house, Gusti. Our one asset, while it lasts. We must make use of it. Get some money into the house.

**Adler**   Oh, not one of your terrible parties!

**Kommer**   One of *his* terrible parties. Money walking round the house and some of it will stick!

**Adler**   We're already entertaining half Salzburg every night of the season!

**Kommer**   Not that Herr Reinhardt often deigns to put in an appearance.

**Adler**   He never knows what to say to people.

**Kommer**   He knows what to say to people when he wants something out of them.

**Adler**   This house was supposed to be a retreat for actors and artists, not a feeding trough for local dignitaries.

**Kommer**   Never mind local dignitaries. Celebrities, Gusti! Bankers who want to meet celebrities! Financiers who want to be celebrities! Money! 'A lordly house and fair' – yes, and this is what it's *for*! The masterpieces on the walls, the flamingos in the garden, the footmen, the maids – this is what it's all leading

up to! To say money! To scream it out − money, money, money!
Money attracts money, Gusti! Money talks to money!

> And so, a fortnight from tonight
> We shall three hundred guests invite,
> And serve the kind of banquet up
> On which financiers might sup.

**Adler**    He so hates entertaining!

**Kommer**    But he loves *rehearsing*! Our own banquet scene!
One of his gigantic productions. We've got the décor. Now all
we need are the extras to dress it.

*Lights down. Gathering rehearsal noise.*

Tables . . . ! Chairs . . . ! Set the sideboard . . . ! Franz! Where
are you, Franz . . . ?

*Enter **Josef** and **Thomas** as peruked footmen, and **Franz**.*

**Kommer**    Maids! Extra maids! Extra footmen! Candles!
Trays!

**Adler**    Maids and footmen, please! Candles! Trays!

*Enter **Liesl**, **Gretl**, and as many understudies as possible, bringing
candelebra, and carrying trays.*

**Adler**    Lights up . . . ! Music . . . !

*Candelebra light. Quartet tunes up.*

And . . . enter God!

*Enter **Reinhardt**. He holds up his hand for silence.*

**Adler**    Quiet, please! Quiet, everyone!

**Reinhardt**
> My aim in life has ever been
> To break the bounds 'twixt world and dream,
> To make the whole world our theatre −
> This house, yes! Nowhere better!
> So let us by the guiles of art
> Create a day that stands apart

From all the grey and shapeless haze
Of unremembered everydays –
That gives a form, a shape, a face
To timeless time and placeless place –
That leaves a sign that we were here
Before Death whispers in our ear.

So – pre-supper positions, please.

**Adler**   Pre-supper positions, everyone!

*The* **Footmen** *and* **Maids** *take up waiting positions with trays.*

**Reinhardt**   Doors open. Guests arriving any minute . . .
Trays high . . . Left hand in small of back . . . Here they come,
here they come. Cue Franz.

*Demonstrates with* **Franz** *announcing the guests.*

**Reinhardt**   'Their Highnesses the Somebodies of
Somewhere . . . His Honour the Somebody of Somewhere
Else . . . '

*He shakes imaginary hands.*

Your Highness! Your Honour . . . ! Serve drinks, serve canapés!

*He rushes the* **Footmen** *and* **Maids** *into action.*

**Reinhardt**   More guests, more guests . . . ! Canapés, drinks!
Keep moving, keep moving . . . Trays high . . . ! Drink, drink,
drink . . . Talk, talk, talk . . . God knows what about, who
cares, keep drinking, keep talking, keep moving . . . And on we
go. Into supper! Cue Franz! Bang bang bang!

**Franz** *and* **Reinhardt** *bang for silence.*

**Reinhardt**   'Your Royal Somethings and Somebodies, Your
This-ships and That-ships . . . Supper is served . . . !' Start
music!

*He demonstrates playing a violin. Musicians off play a minuet. He counts
the bars. On the beat.*

And one . . . two . . . three . . . turn . . . !

*The* **Footmen** *and* **Maids** *turn to face us.*

**Reinhardt**    One . . . two . . . three . . . *move* . . . !

*They move to reform as a line across the stage.*

One . . . two . . . three – *turn* . . . !

*They turn away from us.*

Trays down. *Nap*kins . . . *Plates* . . . *Spoons* . . .

*On the words of command they put napkins over their left arm, and pick up a pair of spoons in their right hand.*

Wait for it, wait for it . . . Dramatic moment . . . And . . . *turn* . . . ! Two . . . three . . . *Move* . . . !

*They advance to a line of imaginary tables.* **Reinhardt** *moves with them, and joins in the actions.*

And . . . *still*! Motionless. Statues . . . Trays up . . . ! Faces like masks . . . Look at Franz's face. He used to serve the Archduke . . . And eyes front again . . . Thank you. Ready to lean . . . Two . . . three . . . *Lean!*

*They all lean deferentially forward.*

Two . . . three . . . *Spoons*!

*They pick up their pairs of spoons.*

And when I say 'show' you show them the first choice on the left of the plate . . . The *left* of the plate . . . Two . . . three . . . *show*!

*They indicate the left-hand choice on the plate with their pairs of spoons.*

Two . . . three . . . Or *how* about *this* . . . ? Or *that* . . . ? Or *this* . . . ? Or *that* . . . ? And now, in your own time . . . *Serve* . . . Good. Good. Well done, five . . . No looking down your nose, two . . . ! Watch Franz . . . Too obsequious, four! Touch of irony! You are playing a part, you are personifying a certain archaic social order. And so are they. And you both know it. And when I say 'Straighten *up* . . . ' Two . . . three . . . Straighten *up*! Two . . . three . . . and step *back* . . . Two . . . three . . . One *place* to the *left*!

*They all take one step sideways to the next imaginary place at table.*

And again from the top. Two . . . three . . . *Lean* . . . ! Two . . . three . . . *Show* . . . ! And on you go . . .

*They repeat the sequence.*

Keep the rhythm going . . . Wonderful . . . Perfect . . . Straighten *up*! Two . . . three . . . and step *back*. Two . . . three . . . And one place to the *left*!

*They repeat the sequence at the next imaginary place along the table, and the next. It becomes a full-scale minuet.*

Plié, rise . . . Plié, rise . . . Left-hand turn . . . Honour your partners . . .

**Kommer** *and* **Adler** *join in.* **Thimig**, **Prince Archbishop**, *and* **Death** *enter from the shadows and join in as well.*

**Reinhardt** *holds up his hand. The music stops.*

**Reinhardt** (*to audience*)
> Dear guests! Before you join us, take
> A well-earned twenty-minute break!

**Adler**
> So, twenty minutes! Don't be late!

**Reinhardt**
> The lady there . . . Your wig's not straight . . .

*The minuet resumes, faster and wilder. Lights down.*

# *Act Two*

*The same.*

*Enter* **Kommer** *and the* **Prince Archbishop**. **Kommer** *gazes down into the auditorium. A murmur of conversation and Mozart.*

**Kommer**
Draw near, good people all, I pray!
Give heed while we perform our play,
Wherein we show, as best we can,
The Summoning of Absolutely Everyman Who is Anyman.

A princess, a grand duke and grand duchess, three American film stars, four leading investment bankers, two of the richest men in Europe, not to mention your good self – and no Reinhardt!

**Prince Archbishop**   So much that Herr Reinhardt has done to this house since he first came here. Surely the greatest of all his celebrated stagings! The statues in the garden . . .

**Kommer**   Carted here complete with a century's growth of moss and lichen on them.

**Prince Archbishop**   The Venetian room . . .

**Kommer**   Transported here, mirror by mirror. The great houses have been stripped for miles around.

**Prince Archbishop**   His wonderful library.

**Kommer**   Copied gallery by gallery from a Swiss monastery. They wouldn't sell! And now all decorated with a better class of extra than he has ever had on a stage before! Look at them down there! Half of them are feeble-minded millionaires who wish for nothing better than to give their millions to some great artistic imposter! But where is the imposter himself? Vanished! It's like putting on one of his great spectaculars and not bothering to sell the tickets! *Is* he a real imposter? We have to ask ourselves! Or is he as feeble-minded as they are?

*Enter* **Müller**.

**Müller**  Look at it all! The corsetmaker's dream of paradise.

**Prince Archbishop**  Now that you and your friends are so prominent in local politics, Herr Müller, you must be grateful to Herr Reinhardt. So much he has done for Salzburg! The whole world comes to the festival.

**Müller**  Gawping holidaymakers. All looking for a quick taste of the spiritual nourishment that Herr Goldmann promised us.

**Prince Archbishop**  Perhaps they find it, Herr Müller.

**Müller**  They watch the play? And they understand the vanity of worldly possessions? They go out and get rid of their money, like Herr Everyman?

**Kommer**  They certainly do! They spend it in the new casino!

**Müller**  And these people. The idle rich of half the world.

**Kommer**  They're also going to be moved to get rid of their money. We hope. To Herr Reinhardt, if we can find him.

**Müller**  And you, Herr Archbishop – are you moved by Herr Goldmann's play?

**Prince Archbishop**  I shed a few tears, I confess, each time I see it.

**Müller**  Touchingly sentimental, all you people in show business. So you've renounced your stipend? You've given up your palace?

**Prince Archbishop**  Ah, Herr Mülller, if you and your friends should ever come to power . . .

**Müller**  We'd have you and Herr Goldmann out on the street as fast as God does Everyman.

*Exit the* **Prince Archbishop** *and* **Müller**. *Enter* **Thimig**.

**Kommer** (*to* **Thimig**)    You've searched the garden? You've
tried the monkey-house . . . ? I'd better go back and keep them
all entertained . . .

*Exit* **Kommer**. **Reinhardt** *emerges from the shadows.*

**Thimig**
Thy guests all wait impatiently
Their dear and gen'rous host to see.
To fetch him thither am I come
With pipe and timbrel, shawm and drum.

**Reinhardt**    They don't need me if they've got Katie. Look
at him down there. He's so much better at being me than I am.
He's fourteen years younger than me. He's still got the energy.
He still believes in it all. The rest of them, though . . . !

**Thimig**    The footmen and maids are giving wonderful
performances.

**Reinhardt**    The guests! Milling helplessly around! They
don't know what they're doing! They haven't been directed!
There's no script, no prompt-book! They don't know what to
say to each other any more than I do!

**Thimig**    They're improvising, Reinhardt.

**Reinhardt**    Improvising! You know what I feel about actors
improvising!

**Thimig**    They're not actors.

**Reinhardt**    No!

**Thimig**    Come on, Reinhardt. You know you've got to go
down there and play your part.

**Reinhardt**    I *am* playing my part. I am watching. I am being
the audience. There is no theatre without an audience. This is
my natural place in life, Leni. In the audience. Looking down
on the world from the gallery. Where I spent my boyhood in
Vienna. Up in the gods at the Burgtheater, wedged in shoulder
to shoulder, looking down on the kings and princes on the
stage. Way, way below. In another world. In a better world.

**Thimig**    For the last thirty years, though, Reinhardt, you've been down there on the stage, rubbing shoulders with the real kings and princess.

**Reinhardt**    And not one of them with the nobility of the kings and princes I saw every night at the Burg. Not one with the ease and assurance of the heroes and heroines I watched when I didn't have the price of a tram to get home. Oh, the great actors of the Burg! They were angels come down on earth! Just the way Lewinsky laid his hat on a chair was worth the walk! Just the way Schratt turned her head! The way your grandfather drank his chocolate!

**Thimig**    They were good at putting their hats down and drinking their chocolate because they were all so old they couldn't remember their lines.

**Reinhardt**    Yes! So the prompter said them first! You heard everything twice!

**Thimig**    You couldn't even see the expressions on their faces from where you were.

**Reinhardt**    So you imagined them for yourself! You played the whole thing out for them inside your head! I breathed with those heroes down there, Leni! I wept with them! I laughed with them! Loved and hated with them! Killed and died with them!

**Thimig**    And then the curtain fell. You came down the stairs from heaven and you started to walk home.

*Enter* **Thomas**, *as the young* **Reinhardt**.

**Reinhardt**    There I go. Back to the Fifteenth District. Or the Eighth, or the Nineteenth, or wherever we are living by this time.

**Thimig**    And gradually . . .

**Reinhardt**    Gradually the air becomes sour with the sour smell of poverty . . .

*Street noise. Trams. Horses. Hurdy-gurdies.*

Street after street. Each one meaner than the last. Tenement
after tenement . . . And up I go. Up the dim, bleak stairs to
the fourth floor, or the third, or the fifth . . . No need for a
prompter here, no need for imagination – you can hear
everything through the walls . . .

*He goes up the stairs. The sounds of children crying, off, and their
mothers screaming at them, the words indistinct; drunken men shouting; the
smashing of crockery; scraps of music being practised over and over again.*

And when I get to our door . . .

*Enter* **Liesl**, *in coat and hat, holding bags and bales.*

**Liesl**    Here – you take the silk. Papa and I will bring the
machine. We've got to be out of here tonight . . .

*Exit* **Liesl** *and* **Thomas**.

**Reinhardt**    So where do I live? Down there, or the Palace
of Elsinore? With a bankrupt corsetmaker and five hungry
brothers and sisters in Vienna 15? Or with Agamemnon in
Argos, with Tamburlaine in Persepolis? Never be homeless,
Leni. Never be poor. Never be an exile. Never play Poor
Neighbour. Never have nothing.

*Enter* **Kommer**.

**Kommer**    And here you are. Of course. In the Burgtheater
again. In the back streets of Vienna. Take him in to supper, if
you please, Fräulein Thimig. You'll find I have seated him next
to Monsieur de Rothschild.

**Reinhardt**    You have invited Rothschild?

**Kommer**    Of course not! *You* have invited Rothschild! You
are the host! I am merely the master of your revels. Since you
don't deign to do the job yourself. And you will not, of course,
play Poor Neighbour . . .

> Now must I kneel to you and plead
> For help in this my hour of need.

If you do you will end up like Poor Neighbour, getting a handful
of small change. It's *Rothschild* who is Poor Neighbour. His hand

out, hoping for a few scraps of charity from the great house of art that you have built. You will be Everyman, gracefully condescending to take him seriously. Only of course you won't show it. Money talking to money. Artist to fellow artist.

**Thimig**    Are you *directing* Herr Reinhardt?

**Kommer**    I *am* directing Herr Reinhardt.

**Thimig**    He *has* talked to money before!

**Reinhardt**    An advisory committee, yes?

**Kommer**    An advisory committee. Could he be persuaded to chair it?

**Reinhardt**    His reputation and his wide range of acquaintance would be invaluable in finding other patrons of the right sort.

**Franz** (*off*)    Your Royal Highnesses, Your Highnesses, Your Lordships and Ladyships, ladies and gentlemen . . . Supper is served.

**Kommer**    Your entrance, Herr Reinhardt!

Once Rothchild shows his smiling face
Our world becomes a better place . . .

*Exit* **Thimig** *and* **Reinhardt**. *Enter* **Müller**.

**Müller**    Look at them all, guzzling the free eats like paupers in a soup kitchen! But Herr Goldmann is right about one thing. A day of reckoning will come. God is not the only one with plans to cleanse the world of its filth. Look at those lights shining up there in the darkness. A new world is being born on that side of the frontier.

**Kommer**    There's still a frontier!

**Müller**    Still a frontier, yes. Between Germans and Austrians. Between Germans and their fellow Germans. Still a frontier.

So! One more day!
Make he wise use of this brief stay!

**Kommer**    The soup kitchen, Herr Müller!

*Exit* **Müller**. *Enter* **Adler** *with the prompt-book.*

**Kommer**    And on we stagger, bailed out for another season.

**Adler**    House, banquet . . .

**Kommer**    Money . . .

**Adler**    Rehearse, play . . . Summer, winter . . .

**Kommer**    Money, money . . .

*Exit* **Kommer**.

**Adler**    Journey . . .

*Enter* **Reinhardt**.

**Adler**    Journey again, Herr Reinhardt?

**Reinhardt**    Journey again.

**Adler**    Journey, please, everyone!

*Exit* **Adler**.

**Reinhardt**    So Death summons Everyman . . .

*He puts on the mask of* **Death**.

> Quick now, make haste, no more delay,
> A long road must thou walk today.
> Thou trav'lest to that far-off land
> Where thou before God's throne shalt stand . . .

And off Everyman has to go. Taking all his comforts in life with him.

*(As* **Everyman**.*)*
> My servants! You! You! – Everyone!
> Out here, and sharp about it! Run!
> I must at once a journey start,
> On foot, with neither coach nor cart.
> The going will be hard indeed,
> And all my people I shall need . . .

Josef! Thomas!

*Enter* **Josef** *and* **Thomas**.

**Reinhardt**
Run back into the house and bring
The trunk I keep my money in!
We must have gold to ease our way,
And tolls and bribes and ransoms pay.

**Josef**
The trunk?

**Thomas**
                    What, not the heavy one?

**Josef**
That stands this high?

**Thomas**
                    And weighs a ton?

**Reinhardt**
Yes! Quickly now! Don't loaf about!
Just pick it up and fetch it out!

*Exit* **Josef** *and* **Thomas**. *Enter* **Thimig**.

**Thimig**   The car's waiting. You've forgotten your lavender water again. And your diamond cufflinks . . .

*Enter* **Franz** *with clothes.*

**Thimig** (*to* **Franz**)   You *have* packed a spare dress suit for Herr Reinhardt?

**Franz**   Also a morning suit, Fräulein Thimig. Just in case. And a small choice of tweeds for the country. One never knows.

*Enter* **Thomas** *and* **Josef**, *carrying with difficulty the trunk we saw earlier.*

**Franz** *packs more clothes in the trunk.* **Reinhardt** *watches.*

**Reinhardt**
Our route lies over unknown ground,
Unknown the land where we are bound.

Heretobefore in evil hours
Some comfort found I in thy powers.
My trunk! I will not go without thee!
I must have mine own things about me!

**Thimig**    You have packed two complete changes of bed
linen? The last time Herr Reinhardt was in London he had to
spend the night sleeping in hotel sheets.

**Franz**    In the trunk, Fräulein Thimig.

**Thimig**    And the feather bed? And the deerskin to go over
the mattress?

**Franz**    All in the trunk, Fräulein Thimig.

**Reinhardt**    Perhaps I don't need the deerskin . . .

**Thimig**    Of course you need the deerskin! You won't sleep
without the deerskin!

**Reinhardt**    The first time I came to Salzburg, when I was
just beginning as an actor, I lived in one small room. In that
one room was everything I needed for my life as a man: a bed,
a cupboard, a table, a washstand, a jug, and a bowl. And into
that one room I carried one small suitcase. In that one suitcase
I had everything I needed for my life as an actor: an evening
suit, a pair of evening shoes, a long black coat, and a pair of
tights. My whole working life, in one small suitcase.

**Josef** and **Thomas** *pick up the trunk.*

**Reinhardt**    One last look round . . .

*They put the trunk down again.*

My wonderful house! Oh God, the baroque is a beautiful
period! In architecture, in music . . . You did order me a
Linzer Torte from Demel . . . ?

**Franz**    With the hams and the cheeses, Herr Reinhardt.

**Reinhardt**    I try to keep things as simple as possible. I travel
with almost no servants at all.

**Franz**    Sir?

**Reinhardt**    Only a valet. But my entire life has become baroque! How has this happened?

**Franz**    Life is not simple, Herr Reinhardt.

**Reinhardt**    Is your life not simple, Franz?

**Franz**    No, Herr Reinhardt.

**Josef** *and* **Thomas** *pick up the trunk.*

**Reinhardt**    Steam iron? Trouser press . . . ?

**Thimig**    Reinhardt, you're going to miss your train!

**Reinhardt** (*to* **Franz**)    At least you don't have to pack frocks and petticoats for me.

**Franz**    No, Herr Reinhardt. Thank you, Herr Reinhardt.

*Exit* **Josef** *and* **Thomas***, with trunk, followed by* **Reinhardt** *and* **Franz***. Enter* **Adler***, carrying telegrams.*

**Adler**    Telegrams, telegrams. Every day they come. Paris, New York . . .

*She hands a batch of them to* **Thimig***.*

London, Rome . . . New York, Brussels, New York . . .

**Thimig** (*reads*)    'Exhausted, depressed . . . ' 'Can't sleep . . . ' 'Superhuman work . . . ' 'Total success . . . ' 'Total despair . . . '

**Adler** (*reads*)    'Repairs to the roof . . . ' 'Money for daughter . . . ' 'Money for nephews, money for nieces . . . '

*Enter* **Kommer***, with more telegrams.*

**Kommer** (*reads*)    Money . . . Money . . . Money again . . .

**Adler**    'How flamingos? How nightingales?'

**Thimig**    'Ecstatic reviews Buffalo.' 'Appalling reviews Cleveland.'

**Kommer**    'Stage rights *Intolerance*.' 'Screenplay *Paradise Lost*.'

*Enter* **Reinhardt***, followed by* **Franz***, and* **Josef** *and* **Thomas** *with the trunk.*

**Reinhardt**    Time, time! No *time* . . . ! Like struggling for breath . . . ! World so rich, life so short . . . ! And on we go, on we go. Dragging my luggage of cares behind me. If I once lie down I shall never get up again . . . Every night – despair . . . Every morning – unpack optimism once again . . .

**Franz** *begins to unpack trunk.*

**Reinhardt**    Wallpaper!

**Franz** (*baffled*)    Wallpaper?

**Reinhardt**    Depressing. Find me another room . . .

**Franz** (*repacks*)    Another room . . .

*Exit* **Reinhardt**, *followed by* **Franz**, *and* **Josef** *and* **Thomas** *with the trunk.*

**Kommer**    'Latvian divorce – '

**Thimig**    We've got it! We've got it!

**Kommer**    ' – not recognised in US!'

**Thimig**    Not divorced?

**Kommer**    'Reno. Trying Reno.'

**Thimig**    'Hamburg. First boat New York.'

**Adler**    Train tickets . . . boat tickets . . . Passport . . . ! Bon voyage . . . !

*Exit* **Thimig**.

**Adler**    'New York. Adaptation Old Testament.'

**Kommer**    'Set four storeys high. Rebuild theatre. Where are you?'

**Adler** (*to* **Kommer**)    Train tickets . . . boat tickets . . . Passport . . . ! Bon voyage . . . !

*Exit* **Kommer**.

**Adler**    'Divorced.' 'Married.' 'Critical triumph.' 'Financial catastrophe.' 'Arriving Salzburg Friday . . . '

*Enter* **Reinhardt** *and* **Thimig**, *followed by* **Franz**, *and* **Josef** *and* **Thomas** *with the trunk.*

**Adler**    Welcome home, Herr Reinhardt! Welcome home . . . *Frau* Reinhardt! So – tell me about the wedding! And the honeymoon! And the Old Testament in New York!

**Reinhardt**    Wonderful. Perfect . . . *Everyman* again, please, Gusti. Prologue . . . House . . . Journey . . . Mammon . . .

**Adler**    Mammon? Mammon, everyone! Mammon emerging from the trunk . . . !

**Reinhardt**    Where is Mammon? Who's playing Mammon?

**Adler**    Oh! There's a problem with his contract!

**Reinhardt**    Katie! Read Mammon . . . ! Where is Katie!

*Enter* **Kommer**.

**Kommer**    Money?

**Reinhardt**    Mammon!

**Kommer**    Mammon?

**Reinhardt**    Get in the trunk!

**Kommer** *climbs into the trunk.*

**Reinhardt**    Wait for the cue. Give him the cue.

**Adler**
'My trunk! I will not go without thee!
I must have mine own things about me!'

**Reinhardt**    Then out you jump.

'Why, Everyman! What should thee ail?
Thy countenance is deathly pale . . . !'

**Kommer**    But . . . New York . . . The theatre . . . The money!

**Reinhardt**    Why is it, Katie, that I have to carry on my back not just all the cares of the house, all the cares of my productions, but the dead weight of *you*, forever carping, forever dragging your feet, forever making difficulties?

*He slams the trunk shut on* **Kommer**.

**Reinhardt**    And on we go. What is the next scene?

*Darkness, and an explosion. Exit* **Reinhardt** *and* **Thimig**. *The lights come up on smoke and broken window.* **Liesl** *and* **Gretl** *sweep up shattered glass.*

**Franz** *ushers in the* **Prince Archbishop**. *Enter* **Thimig** *calmly.*

**Prince Archbishop**    My dear Frau Reinhardt! I have only just heard! Are you unharmed? And Herr Reinhardt – where is Herr Reinhardt?

**Thimig**    Choosing a tie. He would not wish to receive Your Grace in his dressing gown.

**Prince Archbishop**    No one is hurt?

**Thimig**    No one is hurt. Our friends were not very brave. They seem to have simply opened the front door and thrown the bomb inside. The damage is very slight.

**Prince Archbishop**    You didn't catch any sight of them?

**Thimig**    I assume they were the people who did the same to Your Grace's house the other week.

**Prince Archbishop**    We scarcely need to take their attacks on the Church seriously. In your case, however . . .

*Enter* **Reinhardt** *calmly.*

**Prince Archbishop**    My dear boy! My dear boy!

**Reinhardt**    The house will stink of smoke for weeks.

**Prince Archbishop**    Your beautiful house! And there will be worse to come.

**Thimig**    You mustn't worry about us. We have soldiers to escort us to rehearsal each day.

**Prince Archbishop**   They have already taken your great theatre in Berlin . . .

**Reinhardt**   Berlin is in Germany. We are in Austria.

**Prince Archbishop**   Germany is very close.

**Thimig**   Look at it up there! The sun shining on it as if nothing had changed!

**Prince Archbishop**   You take no more interest in politics than I do, Herr Reinhardt. But we both know who is up there in Berchtesgaden looking down on us.

**Reinhardt**   There is still a frontier between us and him.

**Prince Archbishop**   Frontiers can be crossed. Your own speciality, I believe.

**Thimig**   The uncertain frontier between reality and dream.

**Prince Archbishop**   And *that* frontier is one that our neighbour up there has crossed many times. Lines drawn on a map seem to be little hindrance. And when he does come, what will you do? Where will you go?

**Reinhardt**   We have possibilities all over the world. Unlike most people.

**Prince Archbishop**   You will lose everything! Your homeland. Your home.

**Thimig**   We can't even sell it. It's mortgaged, over and over again.

**Prince Archbishop**   You will exchange your house for a suitcase.

**Reinhardt**   I think we have little to fear. As long as you are here to stand by us. As you always have.

**Prince Archbishop**   Yes. As long as I am here. As long as I am here . . .

**Death** (*calls softly, off*)   Everyman!

*The* **Prince Archbishop** *listens.*

**Death**    Everyman!

**Thimig**    Your Grace . . . ?

**Prince Archbishop** (*puzzled*)
Who called? My name! Who called my name?

**Reinhardt**    I heard nothing.

**Thimig**    A bird in the garden, perhaps?

**Reinhardt**    The wind in the trees?

**Prince Archbishop**
From nowhere, everywhere it came . . .

**Reinhardt** *and* **Thimig** *look at each other.*

**Prince Archbishop**
And comes again, and comes again!

**Thimig**    Your Grace! Is Your Grace unwell?

**Reinhardt**    Sit down, Your Grace, sit down. I will telephone
for a doctor.

**Prince Archbishop**    Just have them fetch my car to the
door, if you please, Herr Reinhardt. I have matters to attend to.

**Reinhardt** *hesitates.*

**Prince Archbishop**
I seem to see a strange face there . . .

**Thimig**    Statues, Your Grace. Only the statues.

**Prince Archbishop**
                                                He favours none,
Nor any fears. To all he comes.

**Thimig** *looks at* **Reinhardt**. *He goes.*

**Prince Archbishop**    Will you give me your arm, Frau
Reinhardt? And escort me to my car? I was always a little
saddened to see my hostess leave the house before me, you
know. Touched by your thoughtfulness in sparing my blushes.
But saddened, saddened.

**Thimig**   The Jew's whore.

**Prince Archbishop**   Yes, the Jew's whore. That's what they call you. Even now you're married. Never mind, tonight I shall look back from my car as I leave and I shall see the Jew and his whore standing in the doorway, waving farewell together. And that will be something for me to remember. Something for me to keep in my mind as I lie waiting for sleep.

*Enter* **Reinhardt**.

**Reinhardt**   Your car is waiting. I'm so sorry, Your Grace, I'm so sorry!

**Prince Archbishop**   No need to be sorry for me. I have a home to go to. It's you I worry about.

**Reinhardt**   The suitcase? I'm used to suitcases.

**Prince Archbishop**   After the suitcase.

**Reinhardt**   Another box.

**Prince Archbishop**   Oh, my dear boy, my dear boy!

*He strokes* **Reinhardt**'s *arm.*

**Prince Archbishop**   Believe one thing, even though you believe nothing else: if I could take your place I should.

*The* **Prince Archbishop** *exits on* **Thimig**'s *arm. Darkness.*

**Müller** (*as* **Death**, *off*)
   Everyman! Everyman!

*Twilight.* **Reinhardt** *turns to listen.*

**Müller**
   Thou fool, the stay that thou hast won
   Its little course hath all but run.

*He enters, masked as* **Death**.

   What profit from it hast thou earned
   Now I to find thee am returned?

*He discards his mask*

It was in the props basket. I thought I should enter into the spirit of things. I am after all here as a messenger from on high. (*He indicates.*)

**Reinhardt**    Berchtesgaden?

**Müller**
    While yet of him thou thinkest not,
    He hath not thee likewise forgot.

**Reinhardt**    You know the play.

**Müller**    By heart. Difficult not to, if you live in Salzburg.

**Reinhardt**    And have you come to summon me?

**Müller**    Sooner or later you will have to go on a journey, Herr Reinhardt. Give up all your money. And all your friends. You won't even have your trunk. Or your princely friend to protect you. My condolences on his death. Much loved in some quarters, I know. Particularly by the Jews. Don't despair, though, Herr Goldmann! Remember Herr Everyman! How black things look for him! But he is saved in the end. Escorted into heaven by his Works and his Faith. You have your Works to speak for you, Herr Goldmann. In Berlin the greatest theatre the German people ever had. Another in Vienna. And here in Salzburg you have created a festival that could become a beacon of German culture as bright as Bayreuth. With a little improvement in racial hygiene.

**Reinhardt**    You're not asking me to convert?

**Müller**    You *can't* convert! You can change your beliefs, if you have any. But not your choice of forebears! Not all the generations of the dead! To cease to be a Jew, Herr Goldmann, you would have to be born again as an Aryan.

**Reinhardt**    I don't think I can oblige.

**Müller**    On the contrary, Herr Goldmann. This is what I have been sent here to offer you: the same chance that God offers Everyman. Rebirth!

**Reinhardt**    As an Aryan?

**Müller**    As an honorary Aryan. By the grace of the very
highest authority. (*He indicates Berchtesgaden.*) All you will need is
a little help from Faith. Like Everyman. He finds it difficult at
first to believe in God's mercy.

**Reinhardt**

God smiteth, smiteth! That I know!

**Müller**

Forgiveness also can He show.

**Reinhardt**

Great Pharaoh's host He smote and slew!
Gomorrah smote, and Sodom, too.
Smote! Smote!

**Müller**

Do but believe,
And thou His mercy shalt receive.

**Reinhardt**    There is a price to be paid for this miracle?

**Müller**    Now the real Jew speaks! 'How much does it cost?'
The answer, Herr Goldmann, is – next to nothing. You have a
bargain. You would give up your couple of visits each year to
the synagogue. A few friends and relations. Fräulein Adler and
Herr Kommer, of course. Everything else you can keep. The
house. Your charming new Aryan wife. Congratulations, by the
way! Perfect taste, as in all things. You can go on running the
festival. Go on throwing your parties. Far more generous terms
than Herr Everyman gets! And you have a good chance, unlike
poor Everyman, of being allowed to remain alive.

**Reinhardt** *rings.*

**Müller**    Think about it, Herr Goldmann. The offer will not
remain open indefinitely.

*Enter* **Franz**.

**Reinhardt**    Franz, will you show Herr Müller out?

**Müller**    What's the alternative, Herr Goldmann? To wander,
like your parents, like your forefathers. To become the
Wandering Jew once again.

*Exit* **Reinhardt**.

**Müller** (*to* **Franz**)    And what will happen to you, my friend? Your little room in the attics will vanish with all the rest.

**Franz**    This way, if you please, Herr Müller.

**Müller**    The Wandering Jew – and his wandering shoeshine.

*Exit* **Müller** *and* **Franz**. *Enter* **Thimig**, *carrying a small suitcase, and* **Adler**.

**Adler**    The house is for sale? *This* house? What do you mean?

**Thimig**    It was in the paper. Reinhardt read it in the paper.

**Adler**    How *can* it be for sale? *You're* not selling it!

**Thimig**    The Government is selling it.

**Adler**    Your house? They can't do that!

**Thimig**    Apparently they can. Our debts, Gusti, our debts.

*Enter* **Thomas**, **Josef**, *and* **Franz**, *carrying various items, and* **Reinhardt**.

**Reinhardt** (*to* **Franz**)    And *two* feather beds, of course. We're both going this time! And both our passports . . .

**Adler**    But, Herr Reinhardt – the house!

**Reinhardt**    Money! Only money!

**Adler**    Katie will find a way round it. He always has.

**Thimig**    Katie's in New York already.

**Adler**    I'll cable him to meet you off the boat.

**Reinhardt**    I'm getting tired of Katie. Money is all he ever thinks about. Money and mockery. I can manage without Katie. (*To* **Thomas** *and* **Josef**.) Fetch the rest of the luggage, will you?

*Exit* **Thomas** *and* **Josef**.

**Reinhardt**    Helene – *your* trunk! Where is it?

**Thimig** (*shows the suitcase*)   We're only going for six months. I'm not like you. As long as I've got a Shakespeare and a change of underwear . . . (*To* **Adler**.) You'll keep an eye on the animals?

**Reinhardt**   And my family?

**Thimig**   And the staff?

**Reinhardt**   And the contracts for next season?

**Adler**   Oh, I can't bear this moment! Every autumn! And every autumn it get worse!

**Reinhardt**   We shall be back very soon, Gusti. Like the swallows.

**Adler**   Perhaps this time you won't be.

**Reinhardt**   Of course we shall.

**Thimig**   Shall we?

**Adler**   You won't, you won't! The Archbishop's dead. The Nazis are just waiting for their chance. And now this business with the house . . . Something even worse will happen . . .

**Reinhardt**   Nothing will happen.

**Adler**   Such horrible things everywhere!

**Reinhardt**   Yes . . . And there he waits, up in the gods. Looking down on us all. Another poor boy who has imposed himself on the world. Aping the kings and princes below. Drunk on the possibilities of life.

**Adler**   That vile creature he sent!

**Reinhardt**   Don't worry! By the time we come back all this nonsense will have been forgotten. One last look at our wonderful house . . .

**Thimig**   We used to laugh in this house once. Do you remember that? When we first came here? Everything so shabby and broken down, everything still to be done, and we stood here one night in the middle of it all, and you took my hand, and we both started to laugh . . .

*Exit* **Thimig** *and* **Adler**. *The light changes.* **Reinhardt** *touches the trunk.*

**Reinhardt**
Our route lies over unknown ground,
Unknown the land where we are bound.
Heretobefore in evil hours
Some comfort found I in thy powers.
My trunk! I will not go without thee!
I must have mine own things about me!

*The trunk springs open.* **Kommer**, *as Mammon, rises from it.*

**Kommer**
Why, Everyman! What should thee ail?
Thy countenance is deathly pale!

**Reinhardt**
Who art thou?

**Kommer**
            What, thou dost not know –
And yet with thee wouldst have me go?
Thy wealth am I! Thy worldly all!
Great Mammon, at thy beck and call!
My powers thou knowest. Tell me how
They may be used to serve thee now.

**Reinhardt**
I know not – but most urgently;
A messenger hath come for me.

**Kommer**
A messenger? From whence he came?

**Reinhardt**
Methinks thou knowest, and his name.

**Kommer**
Thy presence elsewhere is desired?

**Reinhardt**
And thine likewise by me required.

**Kommer**

I will not budge from where I stand –
Most happy am I where I am!

**Reinhardt**

Durst thou defy me, durst repine,
Thou creature, thou mere thing of mine?

**Kommer**

Thy thing, thy creature, hast thou said?
The truth thou standest on its head!
I giant-like above thee tower,
Thou like a dwarf canst only cower!

**Reinhardt**

I govern thee and all thou art!

**Kommer**

I rule as king within thy heart!

**Reinhardt**

I king – thou subject of my rule!

**Kommer**

No – I the king and thou my fool!

**Reinhardt**

Thou wert my lowly serving boy!

**Kommer**

And thou my jumping jack, my toy!
This trunk doth thy life's work contain –
And in this trunk it will remain.
Thou goest on thy painful way;
I here at my good ease will stay!

**Kommer** *sinks back into the trunk. The lid falls. Darkness. Exit*
**Reinhardt.**

*Triumphal music. Enter* **Müller**, *wearing a Nazi armband, and*
**Thomas** *and* **Josef**, *also wearing armbands.* **Liesl** *and* **Gretl**
*appear at the front of the stage with flowers.*

**Müller** *(formally)*

Heil Hitler!

**Liesl**, **Gretl** (*and many other voices in the auditorium*)
Heil Hitler!

**Thomas** *and* **Josef** *remove the trunk, then flank* **Müller**.

**Müller**
Now attend to me
While I proclaim my first decree,
Whereby as Gauleiter I ban
All future shows of *Everyman*.
The Jews will now perhaps believe
How short the shrift they will receive,
How firmly we shall use our powers
In this united Reich of ours!

*He comes down the stairs, flanked by* **Thomas** *and* **Josef**, *and becomes relaxed and welcoming*

**Müller**
We shall expropriate the Jew,
And harry his supporters too;
The late Archbishop's grand address
Is now the home of the SS.
While this great palace where we stand –
The lordliest in all the land –
Its owner wisely having fled
Belongs to you and me instead.
Here, as your representative,
I do propose myself to live.
So – make yourself at home! Feel free
To stroll around your property!
Enjoy the gardens, feed the monkeys!
Admire the paintings, tip the flunkeys!
What half so sweet as stolen pleasure?
Or finding someone else's treasure?
The old show ends, the new one starts,
With different management and cast.
One character, though, will remain.
His services we shall retain,
And find him rather more to do.
Our new star, Death, awaits his cue.

*He gives the Nazi salute. Applause from the auditorium. Darkness.*

**Thimig** *opens the blinds, and the light reveals* **Reinhardt**, *asleep at his table.*

**Reinhardt**    Morning? Already?

**Thimig**    Do you want breakfast?

**Reinhardt**    Have I had supper?

**Thimig**    Reinhardt, you will get ill! Then what will become of us? You don't eat! You never go to bed!

**Reinhardt**    I have always worked hard and late. All day and half the night. Always, always.

**Thimig**    But not *all* night, Reinhardt! Not *all* night!

**Reinhardt**    My love, I will never get a movie set up if I don't work! If I don't have a hundred projects to propose! If I don't write outlines and treatments! If I don't draft them and redraft them until I find what the studios want!

**Thimig**    Oh, Reinhardt, this place, this place! If only I could look out of the window one morning and see rain! Veils of rain sweeping across the lake. The mountains lost in clouds. Water dripping from the plants and statues. The whole world soft and grey.

**Reinhardt**    Then you would be saying: 'If only the sun would shine!'

**Thimig**    Yes! 'If only the sun would shine!' If only I could be saying those precious words!

**Reinhardt**    The Pacific is as beautiful as the lake. In its way.

**Thimig**    We are never going back. We are going to die in this awful place. We are never going to see our home again!

**Reinhardt**    Nearly twenty years we lived in that house. Lived in it and lived it! Lived every room.

**Thimig**    Every table.

**Reinhardt**    Every chair, every picture.

**Thimig**  Lived it and gave it life.

**Reinhardt**  Dreamt of it and dreamt it.

**Thimig**  Dreamt it and dreamt it until it was real.

**Reinhardt**  The one production of mine that I thought might endure.

**Thimig**  And we have lost it. We have lost everything that we carried into it.

**Reinhardt**  I will not lament it, though, my love. It's gone – it's past. And we are alive. We are free. We have food to eat, we have clothes to our backs. We have beds to sleep in and a table to work at. I have as much as I had when I first went to Salzburg! And I have you. You didn't have to be here. You could have stayed. Poor Everyman never found anyone to accompany him on his journey. I did. We are together.

*He kisses her hand. Enter* **Adler**, *holding letters.*

**Adler**  I'm sorry . . .

**Reinhardt**  My other faithful companion in exile.

*Kisses her hand.*

The post?

**Adler**  Nothing you need to see.

**Reinhardt**  No money?

**Adler**  No money.

**Reinhardt**  And nothing from Paramount? Nothing from Metro?

**Thimig**  Paramount! Metro! You might as well say fairyland, or heaven!

**Reinhardt**  I am not unknown in this town, my love.

**Thimig**  You made a movie. Once. Seven years ago. In the past! The past is another world! Reinhardt, our only hope is the theatre!

**Adler**    Helene, there is no theatre in Los Angeles!

**Thimig**    There is theatre in New York! At least it sometimes rains in New York! At least New York is halfway home! If I can play Nazis in movies I can play Nazis in plays. In New York.

**Adler**    Helene, they have Nazis in movies. They don't have Nazis in plays.

**Thimig**    And still you always take his side!

**Adler**    No, but Helene, to go to New York –

**Thimig**    – we need money. Money, money, money! If only Katie were here!

**Adler**    But he's *not* here!

**Thimig**    No, because he's in New York already!

**Adler**    If only Herr Reinhardt hadn't fallen out with him!

**Reinhardt**    Katie, though . . . (*Rings.*) Katie – yes! (*Rings.*)

**Adler**    If you could somehow get to New York . . .

**Thimig**    If you could somehow talk to Katie . . .

**Reinhardt**    I don't need to talk to Katie! I talked to Katie for twenty years. For twenty years I put up with him. Long enough to know what he would tell me to do! (*Rings.*)

**Thimig**    What? What would he tell us to do?

**Reinhardt**    Where *is* that valet of mine?

**Thimig**    He's mending the Frigidaire.

**Adler**    He's putting the trash out.

**Reinhardt**    Yes, but he is supposed to be dressing me. (*Rings.*)

*Enter* **Franz**.

**Reinhardt**    Franz, Franz. I must get dressed.

**Franz**    You *are* dressed, Herr Reinhardt.

**Reinhardt**   I *am* dressed. Exactly. I know that . . . But, Franz, Franz – we are going to need your expert services! Because as soon as you mentioned Katie it came to me at once. We must do what Katie always told us to do in the past when things were difficult.

**Thimig**   Spend less? How can we? We don't spend anything!

**Reinhardt**   Give a party!

**Adler**   A party?

**Reinhardt**   Yes! Just the way we used to in the old days! One of our great parties! Invite everyone! All the producers! All the stars! All the big money! 'Mr and Mrs Louis B. Mayer . . . Mr William Randolph Hearst . . . ' This is you, Franz! You remember? 'Miss Betty Grable . . . Mr John Rockefeller Junior . . . '

**Thimig**   But . . . the *money* . . .

**Reinhardt**   Exactly. The money. I take it by the elbow. I admit it into my confidence. Just the way Katie taught me to do. 'So do you feel, Mr Rockefeller, that I should turn Faust into a cowboy or into a gangster . . . ?'

**Thimig**   The money to pay for the party.

**Reinhardt**   I have a little money put by.

**Thimig**   Reinhardt! We have no money put by!

**Reinhardt**   Yes! I know I don't understand money, but I do understand one thing: that everyone must have a last hidden reserve for extreme circumstances.

**Adler** (*shows letters*)   Herr Reinhardt, look! From the bank! Your account!

**Reinhardt**   Cash!

**Thimig**   Cash?

**Reinhardt**   Dollar bills! Carefully hidden away! Precisely so as to keep it from the bank! Precisely so as to stop the bank eating it up!

**Adler**   So . . . how much have you got?

**Reinhardt**   Enough, enough. All I need now is an evening
suit! I began with one evening suit and a pair of tights, and
with one evening suit, even without the tights, I shall begin all
over again. I do still have an evening suit, Franz?

**Franz**   Where it always was, Herr Reinhardt. At the cleaner's,
Herr Reinhardt.

**Reinhardt**   Collect it, then, Franz!

**Franz**   A dollar fifty, Herr Reinhardt.

**Reinhardt**   Take it out of your wages for now, Franz.

**Franz**   What wages, Herr Reinhardt?

**Reinhardt**   Never mind, never mind. Wages, cleaning,
everything – as soon as I've found the money.

**Thimig**   Where is it?

**Reinhardt**   Yes . . . where is it . . . ?

**Thimig**   You haven't forgotten?

**Reinhardt**   Of course I haven't forgotten! I hid it. I hid it
most carefully. I think – yes – in a book.

**Thimig**   In a *book*? Which book?

**Reinhardt**   Which book . . . ? I seem to remember it was
a book with a blue jacket . . . Or a red jacket . . .

**Thimig**   Oh, Reinhardt! Reinhardt, Reinhardt, Reinhardt!

**Reinhardt**   No! I moved it. It's all coming back to me. It's in
my old trunk! Fetch the trunk! We still have the trunk?

*Exit* **Franz**.

**Reinhardt**   Pen and paper! I will draw up a guest list. First
the party. Show everyone we are alive. Begin to set things up.
Then perhaps a season in New York. I will make it up with
Katie. Direct one or two shows. Make our mark. Get our
finances under control.

*Enter* **Franz**, *struggling to carry the trunk single-handed. It is now very battered and shabby.*

**Reinhardt**    Steady, steady! You're not as young as you were! (*He searches in the trunk.*) So, off on my travels again . . . I'm going to need this trunk . . . Deerskin, good . . . Bit moth-eaten . . . The feather bed will have to be aired . . .

**Thimig**    There *is* no money, is there? There never was. You just imagined it . . .

**Reinhardt** (*holds up a loose heap of dollar bills*)    I'm going to give it to Gusti to look after.

*He hands her the money.*

**Reinhardt**    Gusti – you will be responsible for paying the caterer and hiring the musicians and buying the train tickets and paying Franz . . . Franz, take *everything* in here to the cleaner's. A completely fresh start . . .

**Franz** *packs everything back into the trunk and takes it off.*

**Reinhardt** (*to* **Adler**)    You are also responsible for paying the cleaner's. And you will be as careful with the money as you always are – as careful as Katie would be – as careful as my poor brother was – because you will remember that what you are holding in your hands is our lifeline. Our last hope. Now, shave. A good confident suit . . .

*Exit* **Reinhardt**.

**Thimig** (*to* **Adler**)    How much is it?

**Adler** (*counts it*)    Seventeen dollars.

*Exit* **Thimig** *and* **Adler**. *Enter* **Kommer**, *together with* **Thomas**, **Josef**, **Liesl** *and* **Gretl** *as fellow exiles.*

**Kommer**    Seventeen dollars! His life savings!

**Thomas**    So – no party?

**Kommer**    On seventeen dollars?

**Liesl**    And no Katie to make it go?

**Josef**   You know he's here?

**Thomas**   In New York?

**Liesl**   Got here from LA?

**Thomas**   On seventeen dollars?

**Josef**   Sold the furniture, I gather.

**Gretl**   Had to leave Helene behind!

**Josef**   What – minding the shop?

**Liesl**   Poor Helene!

*Enter* **Reinhardt**. **Kommer** *and the other exiles watch him, like* **Reinhardt** *and* **Thimig** *watching the party earlier.*

**Gretl**   Poor Reinhardt!

**Thomas**   So he's all alone?

**Kommer**   All alone? Reinhardt?

*Enter* **Franz** *carrying the trunk.*

**Reinhardt** (*to* **Franz**)   Careful, careful! No point in saving money on porters if you end up in hospital . . . Is this the only room you could get? Where is the sky? Where are the trees?

**Franz**   We are in the middle of Manhattan, Herr Reinhardt!

**Reinhardt**   What was wrong with the hotel we were in before?

**Franz**   We hadn't paid the bill, Herr Reinhardt.

**Kommer** (*to* **Thomas** *and the other exiles*)   It's like a play I remember seeing.

**Liesl**   A man who has everything.

**Gretl**   Money, friends, a beautiful home.

**Josef**   And then – pfft!

**Thomas**   It's all vanished.

**Kommer**    Forty-fifth Street – coming along the sidewalk – there he was. Eyes down. So aged. So anxious . . . He looked up and saw me. I know he saw me . . .

**Reinhardt** (*to* **Franz**)    My address book . . . What have you done with my address book . . . ? I must set up some meetings. Producers, agents . . . People I've worked with in the past – they won't have forgotten me . . .

**Kommer**    For twenty years I put up with that man. For twenty years I kept a warm feather bed of money and friends around him . . . If he'd so much as shaken my hand! So much as nodded and smiled! I could have tried to do something.

**Liesl**    Poor Reinhardt!

**Kommer**    Poor us! Poor all of us! None of us knowing where next week's rent is coming from.

**Josef**    Exiles.

**Kommer**    The wrong language, the wrong style, the wrong friends. All reduced to playing the same part.

>   Now must I kneel to you and plead
>   For help in this my hour of need . . .

And who are we kneeling and pleading to? Anyone we can find who understands us. Other exiles. Other Poor Neighbours as desperate as ourself.

**Reinhardt** (*to* **Franz**)    And yes, they want me, they want me! Broadway again, Franz! A big musical! Contracts almost ready to be signed! The money almost in place!

**Kommer**    And he's fourteen years older than me. Not long now before he hears the voice whispering from the shadows . . .

**Death** (*off, whispers*)    Everyman!

**Kommer**    And there it is!

**Death**    Everyman!

**Kommer**    You hear it?

**Thomas**, **Josef**, **Liesl**, *and* **Gretl** *turn to look at* **Kommer**.

**Kommer**    Look! Look! There! Standing in the shadows . . . !

*The others begin to melt discreetly away.*

**Kommer**    *He* can hear it, though! *He* can see it . . . ! Can't he?

**Reinhardt** (*to* **Franz**)    I have meetings to go to. The money, of course, the money. As always! Money, money . . .

*Darkness begins to close in around* **Kommer**.

**Kommer**    Poor old soul! He must be deaf already, his eyesight must be failing . . . (*Becomes aware that he is alone in the gathering darkness.*)

**Death** (*off*)    Everyman!

**Kommer**    Or *me*, then? *My* story all the time? *Me* who's Everyman?

**Reinhardt**    And get Katie on the phone for me. Never too late to mend a quarrel. Poor devil. I might be able to find him something . . .

**Franz** *picks up the phone.*

**Kommer**    Of course! Always a last twist in the plot! Only now I shall never find the answer to my question. Is he feeble-minded, or is he an imposter? Or both? Or is he just possibly something else altogether . . . ?

*The darkness swallows* **Kommer** *up. Now only* **Reinhardt** *and* **Franz** *are lit.* **Franz** *listens for a moment, then puts down the receiver. He crosses himself.*

**Reinhardt**    No! Even Katie . . . ? Poor Katie. However did I put up with him for all those years? Never mind. We don't need Katie. I can manage without Katie . . . But this suit, Franz, this suit! I'm an old man in this suit! I cannot meet money looking like this!

**Franz**    A summer jacket, perhaps, Herr Reinhardt?

**Reinhardt**    A summer jacket . . . Quickly, then.

**Franz** *fetches the jacket.*

**Reinhardt**    I can't play an old man again. I played old men when I was twenty. I was good at it then . . .

*He holds out his right arm for **Franz** to put the summer jacket on, but then cannot get his left arm back for the other sleeve.*

**Reinhardt**    Help me, then, Franz, help me . . . ! What are you doing . . . ?

**Franz**    Your arm, Herr Reinhardt . . .

**Reinhardt**    I can't . . . I can't . . . I can't . . . Help me – I . . . Help me – I . . . Help me . . . !

**Franz** *drops the jacket and runs to the phone.*

**Reinhardt**    No! No! Not ill! No! No! Or money won't . . . Money won't . . . Money won't . . . Money . . . Money . . .

**Death** (*whispers, off*)
　　Everyman! Everyman!

*Darkness. Only **Reinhardt** remains lit.*

**Reinhardt**
　　So . . . my name now! In my own ears
　　The voice that only one man hears.

**Death** *emerges from the darkness.*

**Death** (*whispers*)
　　Everyman! Everyman!

**Reinhardt**
　　For me it comes, the pale face there.
　　At me those eyes so coldly stare.

**Death**
　　God smiteth, smiteth! Smiteth all!
　　Like grass before the scythe they fall.
　　Thy brother smote He – smote and slew!
　　The Prince Archbishop. Katie, too.
　　Smote! Smote! And smiteth still,
　　Until the grey cold graveyards fill.

**Reinhardt**
> Farewell, my shabby trunk, at last!
> My dwindling treasure of things past!
> Now down into the grave I go,
> Down, down into the dark below.

*Enter* **Thimig**.

**Thimig**
> Thy Faith by thee will faithful stand.

*Enter* **Adler**.

**Adler**
> And I, thy Works, at thy right hand.

**Thimig**
> Before his Judge he goeth, shorn
> Of all he got since he was born.

**Adler**
> No riches hath he but the sum
> Of what he hath believed and done.

**Reinhardt**
> One day of birth, one day of death!
> I tried, as long as I drew breath,
> To melt the frontiers between
> The world we know, the world we dream,
> The things we are, the things we could be –
> And what we would be! – What we should be!
> With art and craft I sought to breach
> The walls dividing each from each.
> My faith? My deeds? I strove to give
> Us mortals other lives to live . . .

*A grave opens in front of* **Reinhardt**, *and he goes down into it.*

**Adler**
> When man ends his allotted days,
> To God, man's maker, Jews give praise.

**Thimig**
> And so to man is tribute paid,
> For maker is what maker made.

*Darkness.*

*Lights up at once.* **Kommer, Thimig, Adler, Prince Archbishop, Thomas, Josef, Liesl, Gretl** *and* **Franz. Kommer** *has just opened a bottle of champagne.* **Thomas, Josef, Franz, Liesl,** *and* **Gretl** *serve drinks and refreshments.*

**Kommer**
> Our play is ended, as plays must,
> And Everyman returned to dust.

**Adler**
> At funerals we weep, but after . . .

**Thimig**
> We raise a glass and turn to laughter.

**Kommer**
> So one last party let us throw,
> Like all those others, long ago . . .

**Prince Archbishop**
> An epilogue to end the show,
> And homeward cheerful make us go.

**Kommer**
> Draw near, good people all, I pray!
> Max Reinhardt is at home today!

*Enter* **Reinhardt.**

**Thimig**
> To Max, our Everyman!

**Adler**                          And then . . .

**Reinhardt**
> To all the other Everymen!

**Prince Archbishop**
> The prince who did this house erect . . .

**Franz**
His bricklayers, his architect . . .

**Prince Archbishop**
The prince who used his high position
To help a wandering musician . . .

**Thomas**
Their footmen . . .

**Josef**
     Gard'ners . . .

**Liesl**
        Maids . . .

**Gretl**
          And cooks . . .

**Adler**
The inky clerks who kept their books . . .

**Kommer**
And carefully nurtured all their wealth . . .

**Reinhardt**
Poor scribbling Amadeus himself . . .

**Thimig**
And us! And us! Who laboured since
To serve our later, greater prince.

**Adler**
We too, each in our turn, we all
Have that same secret voice heard call.

**Prince Archbishop**
We all have that same journey made,
Alone and friendless and afraid.

*Enter* **Death**.

**Death**
To all I come, in many guises,
Yet still the sight of me surprises.

And, in my eagerness to please,
Too many sometimes do I seize.
Then even I must turn and see
A shadowed figure watching me.

**Reinhardt** (*as God, off*)
Where art thou, Death? Thee, too, I call!
Come forth!

**Thomas** *and* **Josef** *seize* **Death** *and rush him forward.*

**Reinhardt**
        Unmask!

*They rip off* **Death**'s *mask and cloak, to reveal* **Müller** *in his Nazi armband.*

**Reinhardt**
        Before me fall!

*They hang him.*

**Prince Archbishop**
God took us all.

**Kommer**
        And yet not so!
We live on still with you below!

**Reinhardt**
Look! Here's the house in all its glory!
High storey still on noble storey!

**Thimig**
Still flowers the garden every spring,
The fountains play, the blackbirds sing.

**Prince Archbishop**
And Amadeus?

**Thimig**
        Every song
He ever sang lives on, lives on.

**Kommer**
And even Death, so I've heard tell . . .

**Death** *appears in the shadows.*

**Death**
Alive and well, alive and well.

**Thimig**
And us? The partners in the dance?

**Adler**
Helene . . .

**Thimig**
         Gusti . . .

**Adler**
                Katie . . .

**Kommer**
                        Franz . . .

**Franz**
Herr Reinhardt . . .

**Reinhardt**
                His High Princely Grace.

**Prince Archbishop**
Well, here we stand, one last faint trace.

**Thimig**
We're only matchstick men, you say . . .

**Adler**
Mere scarecrows stuffed with musty hay . . .

**Kommer**
A grinning turnip for a head . . .

**Prince Archbishop**
Tricked out with words we never said . . .

**Franz**
A tinsel touch of ragged rhyme . . .

**Reinhardt**
Bare shreds left by the winds of time . . .

**Thimig**
Mere made-up things, mere Everymen . . .

**Adler**
Like Everyman himself.

**Kommer**
                        But then
Whate'er our faults, whate'er our merit,
We are the world that you inherit.

**Thimig**
The actors pass, the lines remain.

**Prince Archbishop**
This year in Salzburg once again . . .

**Adler**
The summer sunlight comes and goes . . .

**Thimig**
The pigeons whirr, the cold wind blows . . .

**Adler**
The old expectant silence falls . . .

**Thimig**
And once again that same voice calls:

**Reinhardt**
Draw near, good people all, I pray!
Give heed while we perform our play,
Wherein we show, as best we can,
The Summoning of Everyman . . .

*Lights down.*

# POSTSCRIPT

The genesis of this play was its setting – Schloss Leopoldskron, the great baroque palace on the outskirts of Salzburg.

It is by any standards what an estate agent would call an imposing residence. It was built in the middle of the eighteenth century by the Prince Archbishop of Salzburg, and its white stucco façades, in the Austrian rococo style, crowned by the Prince Archbishop's coat of arms, give it the appearance of an enormous wedding-cake. It looks northwards towards the Festung, the great fortress that dominates Salzburg, southwards across a lake towards the even vaster backdrop of the Alps.

A huge portrait of its builder, Prince Archbishop Leopold Anton Freiherr von Firmian (one of whose successors, a few years later, was the patron of the young Mozart), hangs in the galleried Marble Hall of the Schloss. It looks down now upon the scholars who come from all over the world to attend the academic conferences organised by the present occupants of the palace, the Salzburg Seminar. I stayed there with my wife, who was speaking at one of them, and I was astonished to discover that for eighteen years, from 1920 until 1938, this princely establishment had been the private home of someone who was in a sense a professional colleague of mine – the great Austrian producer and director Max Reinhardt.

There is a theatricality about all baroque and rococo architecture, and the perfect setting of Leopoldskron almost suggests a painted backcloth. I could see why it might have appealed to a man of the theatre. The sheer scale of it, though, indicated a breathtaking level of social grandeur. There have been many princes (and princesses) of the entertainments industry, from the nineteenth century onwards, who have housed themselves pretty lavishly, but even by the most extravagant standards of show business Leopoldskron seemed remarkable – particularly when I discovered that Reinhardt had owned two other properties at the same time – one, in Berlin, a wing of the Bellevue Palace, the official residence of the former German Crown Prince (and now of the Federal President), and the other, in Vienna, an apartment in the Hofburg, the official residence of the former Austrian Emperor.

The theatre is a notoriously uncertain way of earning a living, and it's always encouraging to find that there are at any rate some people in the business who have managed to keep their heads above water. Reinhardt had been able not only to buy the palace and maintain it in the style to which it was accustomed but to go far beyond. When he acquired it, in 1918, it was in a sadly decayed state, and he devoted himself to restoring it – then went on to raise it to heights of glory that it had never known, even in the days of Firmian. It was his passion. He ransacked the great houses of Austria and south Germany for statuary and pictures – transshipped complete rooms – scoured Europe for antique furniture and books – filled the gardens with exotic plants and creatures – employed the finest craftsmen to carve and gild, to refurbish and replace, to copy the furnishings that could not be bought. Of all his many productions, said Helene Thimig, his companion and eventually his second wife, Leopoldskron was the one he was proudest of. Reinhardt and Thimig had no children together. Leopoldskron was their child, and together they loved it and nurtured it with parental intensity.

And then they lost it.

Reinhardt had made an unwitting early mistake in life that had re-emerged, as in a Greek tragedy, to break him. He had been born a Jew. In 1938, when Hitler absorbed Austria into the German Reich, Leopoldskron was 'aryanised' – expropriated – and Reinhardt was forced into exile.

As my wife and I walked through the gardens that Reinhardt and Thimig had created, she read out to me, from the Seminar's brochure on the history of Leopoldskron, this paragraph in a letter he wrote to Thimig in 1942, the year before he died:

> I have lived in Leopoldskron for eighteen years, truly lived, and I have brought it to life. I have lived every room, every table, every chair, every light, every picture. I have built, designed, decorated, planted and I have dreamt of it when I was not there. I have always loved it in a festive way, not as something ordinary. Those were my most beautiful, prolific and mature years . . . I have lost it without lamenting. I have lost everything that I carried into it. It was the harvest of my life's work.

I was moved by this noble expression of resignation. I walked straight into the centre of Salzburg and bought all the books relating to Reinhardt that I could find.

*

Max Reinhardt today is probably not much remembered outside Germany and Austria. I asked a number of normally well-informed friends in London if they knew anything about him. One recalled the British publisher of the same name. Most of the others confessed ignorance. For the first forty years of the twentieth century, though, he was a world celebrity.

Outside the German-speaking lands his reputation derived partly from a legendary *Midsummer Night's Dream* which he staged in various places, and which eventually became a Hollywood film (his only one), with the young Mickey Rooney as Puck. He was probably known mostly, though, for his spectacular international stagings of a play called *The Miracle*. This (as even serious theatre historians may now need to be reminded) was the story of a medieval nun who falls in love with a knight, and is first abducted from her nunnery and then abandoned by him. But God takes pity on her and sends a miracle. A statue of the Virgin comes to life and takes on the identity of the fallen sister to conceal her absence.

This heart-warming tale was told with a lavishness that far outdid any modern musical or rock show. The Vienna production in 1912 had a cast of 1,500 and an orchestra of 150, the London one a cast of 2,000 and and orchestra of 200. In New York in 1924 the parts of the Nun and the Virgin were alternated between two noted society beauties – Lady Diana Duff Cooper representing the British aristocracy and Rosamond Pinchot its American equivalent. (The latter, like the Nun, went to the bad, apparently as a result of her sudden stardom. The Virgin in this case failed to intervene, and she ended up taking her own life.)

In 1937 Reinhardt outdid this with an even more stunning excursion into show-business piety – this time Judaic rather than Christian, a Broadway show called *The Eternal Road*, which covered the entire history of the Jews, through the forty

centuries of the Old Testament and on through the twenty
centuries of the Diaspora. It's true that it had only a modest
cast – 350 – but between them they wore 1,700 costumes, and
the sets, which were four storeys high and covered almost an
acre, required the rebuilding of the theatre. The result was a
sellout – and beggared all who had been cajoled to invest in it.

Before the First World War Reinhardt was said to be the
third most popular personality in Germany after the Kaiser
and Count Zeppelin, and in Germany and his native Austria
his name remains a familiar one. The tide of theatrical fashion,
though, long ago turned against him and everything he
represented, in favour of the kind of theatre associated with
Brecht and Piscator. Even at the height of his success he was
often dismissed as a mere showman, and his son Gottfried
accepts, in his memoir of his father, that 'a slight whiff of
charlatanism' has always hovered about him. Some commentators
on the German theatre, however, now believe that there are
signs of a reassessment.

And so, it seems to me, there should be. The spiritual force
of his great religious extravaganzas may have become a little
dimmed by time, but his real achievements were on no less
a scale. In 1905 he took over the direction of the Deutsches
Theater in Berlin, rebuilt it, and bought out its previous owner.
Without any state or city subsidy he turned it into an institution
that, in its scope, ambition, and output, came to occupy the
same kind of position that the National Theatre now does in
London. He did the great classics, and he introduced the most
interesting new writers of the day to German audiences –
Chekhov, Ibsen, Strindberg, Pirandello, Shaw, Galsworthy,
Hauptmann. By the time he gave up the running of the theatre
in 1932 it had produced over 450 plays – and he had directed
about 170 of them himself. It was the only private art theatre
in the world, he claimed, that had managed to support itself,
without subsidy and without political or party connection, out
of its own resources.

His energy and ambition were boundless. In 1923 he took
on, in addition to the Deutsches Theater, the lease of the
beautiful Theater in der Josefstadt in Vienna, and did for his
native city what he had already done for Berlin. By this time

he had also helped found the Salzburg Festival, in the teeth of considerable local reluctance, and was responsible for all the drama that was produced there. By the end of his life he had directed some 340 productions and built or rebuilt no less than thirteen theatres.

\*

He was born Max Goldmann, in 1873. The Goldmann family had for generations eked out a modest living as small businessmen in the little town of Stampfen (aka Stomfa, aka Stupava, depending upon which of the local languages was in the ascendant) near Pressburg (aka Bratislava), then in Hungary, in a district which had served historically as a dumping ground for Jews driven out of Austria on the other side of the Danube. By the middle of the nineteenth century, though, the Jews of Austria had been emancipated – and the German-speaking Jews of Hungary subjected to pogroms and forced magyarisation. In1869 Max's father moved to Vienna, where he set up a firm trading in cotton goods and married a woman from Moravia. At first the business seems to have prospered, but by the time Max, their first child, was born, the stock market had collapsed, the firm had gone bankrupt, and the Goldmanns had had to move into more modest quarters. As the family grew so its fortunes declined. Another bankruptcy followed. Max's father sold bed springs and bedding feathers for someone else; took over the business; went bankrupt again; became a corset-maker. In the course of Max's childhood the family moved seven times. At the end of his life, after he had lost everything and was struggling to survive in exile, Reinhardt said that he had gone through the torment of sudden impoverishment before, in his parents' home as a child. It was, he said, incomparably worse than poverty itself.

From this shifting and straitened world he escaped into the theatre. When he wrote later, as he often did, about his boyhood passion for the Burgtheater, the vast imperial court theatre of Vienna (claimed to be the second oldest in the world after the Comédie Française), you get the feeling that he saw it as providing him with not just an alternative world to inhabit for a few hours in the evening but a complete alternative biography. 'I always say that I was born in the gods. There I saw for the first time the light of the stage. There I was nourished (for forty crowns an evening) on the rich artistic fare of the Imperial-Royal institution, and there the famous actors of the day sang their classic speech-arias around my cradle.' In Vienna at the time, he says, theatre was based exclusively on the spoken word. 'The stage was completely primitive, there were the bare necessities of furniture; everything else was the actor and his word . . . The Burgtheater was full of voices, that formed an incomparably well-toning orchestra, like old and precious instruments.'

He goes on to give a brilliantly evocative account of the excitement that theatre can sometimes generate:

> The sound came to us out of the remote distance, pressed together as we were, up in the highest point of the house . . . My neighbours . . . were almost exclusively young people . . . I knew no one among them and in any case little was said. It was much too exciting . . .
>
> As soon as it got dark and the curtain rose we melted together into one mysterious unity . . . Suddenly 250 faces broke into a single smile, then a giggle ran through the rows of people – and suddenly a ringing laugh broke out like a storm. You were swept irresistibly away, and you rejoiced that all the others were as drunk on merriment as you were. Then gradually it would become quieter and ever more still. The actors heard every stirring, just as we heard theirs. They would wait until we had settled . . . Things would become serious. Hundreds bent to the left, where someone had entered. The couple on the stage didn't see him. We were in the secret. Hearts beating. Breathing in time together. Two companies: the company of actors and the company of the audience.

The actors at the Burg tended to be elderly, and Reinhardt describes how they forgot their lines and had to be prompted – and were so remote that you could scarcely see them. But even this he saw as a kind of virtue. It meant that 'you had to play along with them yourself up there. The distance from the stage was so great . . . that you had to fill everything out for yourself.'

He saw them as the real rulers of Vienna. 'The way they dressed influenced the way the aristocracy dressed. When one of the actors drank chocolate on the stage people watched with bated breath.' At the age of seventeen he became an actor himself, and adopted a new name, 'Reinhardt', to go with the new persona he was creating; and he became rather famous at the age of twenty, perhaps as a result of watching all those ancients at the Burg, for his ability to glue on a false beard and become an old man.

He worked in small theatres around Vienna, and in 1894 played a summer season in Salzburg. It was here that he got his first big break – a contract to join Otto Brahm's company in Berlin that autumn. Berlin was a relatively new theatrical centre, and Brahm was establishing for the first time its pre-eminence over Vienna. He had taken over the direction of the Deutsches Theater, accommodated in an old operetta house and now having a *succès de scandale* with the innovative naturalism of productions that introduced middle-class audiences for the first time to the social realities of poverty and sexual hypocrisy (Hauptmann's *The Weavers*, for example, and Ibsen's *Ghosts*).

Reinhardt's feelings about the revolution in which he now began to play a part were mixed. 'I was always acting in torn clothes, dirty and smeared,' he wrote later. 'Night after night I had to eat sauerkraut on stage. I wanted for once to play something else as well, something more beautiful and more enjoyable. At that time we had a club with merry and talented members. We allowed ourselves a good deal of professional fun at the expense of all the gloom in the art we practised.' The mockery was channelled into a kind of satirical cabaret, *Schall und Rauch* (Sound and Smoke – i.e. appearance without substance), which fought a running battle against the censors and was a great popular success. The team took over a small theatre to house the shows, and went on to produce first one-act straight plays in it, then full-length ones. Although one of these, Wilde's *Salome*, was seen as marking a decisive break with naturalism, it was a naturalistic production that propelled Reinhardt to the next stage of his career. He read about the opening of Gorky's *The Lower Depths* at the Moscow Art

Theatre, sent a friend to Russia to see it and fetch the text,
then produced it with such enormous success that he was able
to take over a second theatre as well.

Here, in the Neues Theater in 1905, he first did the
*Midsummer Night's Dream* that he was to direct over and over
again in the following years, and that became the signature
of his style. The production of a play is an event in time that
vanishes once the run is over as surely as youth or summer,
and it is impossible to reconstruct it or to know why it should
have caught the audience's imagination. As Gottfried Reinhardt
recalls in his memoir of his father, the play itself was only too
familiar in Germany, where it was regarded as a rather tedious
fairy-tale fit only for school matinees.

'What had made this tired warhorse a winning racer?' he
asks. 'How could this drug on the repertory market suddenly
transform itself into a smash hit and make its producer
Europe's number one theatre man?' Not the text, evidently,
nor even Mendelssohn's music, which had already been used
to accompany many German productions. Not the actors,
excellent as they were, nor the set, even though it was based
on the novelty of a revolving stage. 'It was the *sum total* of all
these elements,' says Gottfried, in a striking passage of critical
description, 'or, to put it another way, the new element that
made out of all of them a conceptual whole; the single idea to
which all participants bent plus the generating force behind
them; the unfamiliar ingredient of a new type of *direction*. The
woods *acted*. The actors were a botanical part of the woods.
Trees, shrubbery, mist, moonlight intermingled with the lovers,
the rehearsing artisans, the trolls, the elfs, the spirits. The
music, the wind, the breathless running, the clowning, the
fighting were all of one key and came from one and the same
source. So did the calm, the sweep, the dream, the poetry.
Nothing was background, nothing foreground. Passion, humour,
lyricism, bawdiness, nobility, fantasy did not have their allotted
moments side by side or consecutively. They were ever-present,
simultaneous, feeding on one another in multiple symbiosis.'

To achieve this, Reinhardt exercised total control over
everything, including the actors' performances. In the
autobiographical notes that he wrote later in his life he

describes how he worked, reading and working over a text
until . . .

> Finally you have a complete optical and acoustic vision. You see
> every gesture, every step, every piece of furniture, the light, you
> hear every intonation, every rise in emotional temperature, the
> musicality of the idioms, the pauses, the different tempi. You feel
> every inward stirring, you know how it is to be concealed and
> when it is to be revealed. You hear every sob, every intake of
> breath. The way another character listens, every noise onstage
> and backstage. The influence of light.
>
> And then you write it down, the complete optical and acoustic
> vision, like a score. You can scarcely keep up, so powerfully are
> you driven, mysteriously in fact, without discussion, without labour.
> Justification you find later. You write it chiefly for yourself. You
> have no idea why you see and hear it this way or that. Difficult to
> write down. No notation for speech. You invent your own signs.

I've never met any modern director who works like this. But
then nor have I met one who wears the kind of clothes in
which Thimig dressed Reinhardt – handmade suits of
tastefully restrained grey English flannel (though Michael
Blakemore, who has directed so many of my plays, including
*Afterlife*, wears handmade shoes). The style has changed. Styles
of dressing and directing, as of everything else, come and go.
Alan Bennett, in *Writing Home*, remembers when he was a boy
in Leeds seeing members of the Yorkshire Symphony Orchestra
going home on the tram after the concert, 'rather shabby and
ordinary and often with tab ends in their mouths, worlds away
from the Delius, Walton and Brahms which they had been
playing. It was a first lesson to me that art doesn't have much
to do with appearances and that ordinary middle-aged men in
raincoats can be instruments of the sublime.' So, on occasion,
can extraordinary men in handmade suits.

As Reinhardt's notes on his methods continue, and he
begins work in the rehearsal room, he sounds for a moment as
if he is prepared to set his carefully prepared battle plans aside
and to work collaboratively with the actors, as most modern
directors do, in a joint effort to discover what the text has to

offer. 'You talk to the actors about their parts,' he says. 'You listen, you get new ideas . . . Some actors have their own ideas. They insist on playing cheerful devils as fallen angels. Tragically, magnificently. You nod in an interested way, agreeing with them.' This collaboration, however, soon turns out to be not quite what it seems. 'The individual opinions rarely have any importance,' he says, 'but you take them seriously. You allow yourself to be convinced.'

Modern directors, of course, also feign deference in this way more often than they would be prepared to admit. Once rehearsals begin in earnest, though, Reinhardt's methods are again quite openly autocratic. 'You play all the parts,' he says. This is something that no modern director, in my experience, would dare to attempt. According to Thimig in her biography of her husband, however, it is precisely what Reinhardt's actors loved about him – that at rehearsals he was himself an actor, and one who could demonstrate every kind of part – old men (of course) but also 'children, eccentrics, women, girls, and lovers'. One actor who worked with him remembers him having the same line line repeated over and over again, then saying it over and over again himself; another as guiding the player, 'without saying much, on invisible threads. With a look, a nod of the head, and then with one or two brief words, he leads him where he wants.' Then, when it comes to bringing an ensemble scene to life, 'he jumps in himself, takes actors waiting for their entrance by the hand, rushes them forwards into the middle of the stage, throws them (in one rehearsal it did actually happen) down on their knees, raises their hands – in a word, is now the leader who rushes into the battle ahead of everyone.'

One of Reinhardt's innovations, after he had moved on to the Deutsches Theater, had perhaps a more profound influence than even the revolving stage that he had introduced in *A Midsummer Night's Dream*: he added to the main house a studio theatre, the Kammerspiele. The auditorium of this smaller house comprised 292 seats – little bigger than the stage, and separated from it only by a couple of steps. This smallness and closeness allowed actors to develop a more intimate style, better suited to the new plays that Reinhardt was doing. It also created a luxuriously furnished space, closed off from the outside world, in which actors and audience felt themselves to be a single entity. 'Since I first came into the theatre,' wrote Reinhardt in a letter to Thimig, 'I was pursued and finally guided by one clear thought: to bring actors and audience together – pressed up against each other as closely as possible. Why? Theatre consists in essence of both these partners.'

Most major producing theatres now have a Kammerspiele of one sort or another attached, and in them (particularly in the National Theatre's Cottesloe) some of my best evenings in the theatre have been spent (and some of the best productions of my own plays done). Reinhardt himself, though, later changed his mind. 'I found that it was all a mistake,' he wrote in his autobiographical notes. 'The small house, the nearness of the stage, the all-too-comfortable seats. The Kammerspiele held too few people, and the quality of the audience grows with its quantity.' And also declines with its metropolitan sophistication. 'The so-called "good" audience is in reality the worst. Dulled unnaive people. Unobservant, blasé . . . Only the gallery is good.'

He seemed to be hankering for the kind of theatre that had first captured his imagination as a child in Vienna. But he went further. He turned his back, as other directors did later, on the concept of theatre as illusion, as an animated peepshow. His intentions remained the same: to dissolve the traditional boundaries between stage and house, and to involve the audience, the essential second company in which he had himself so memorably played at the Burgtheater. But now he thought that it could best be done as it had been in classical Greece, or in the medieval marketplace – by creating dramas that served as religious, or quasi-religious, experiences for a mass audience in a vast open arena. He conceived the idea of the 'Theatre of the Five Thousand', whose numbers were to be drawn not from *die oberen Zehntausend*, as the upper crust are called in Germany (and who, if they have been counted correctly and had all bought tickets, could presumably have supported only two performances of a production) but from the ranks of 'upwardly-striving workers and craftsmen' hungry for art and culture.

He tried the idea out at a summer festival in Munich in 1910, with a production of *Oedipus Rex*, in a new adaptation by Hugo von Hofmannsthal, before an audience of three thousand. The experiment was judged a success (though quite how many of the audience were upwardly-striving workers is not clear). He took over a 3,000-seat circus hall in Berlin and moved the production in, then next year followed it up with the *Oresteia*. That December he found time to go to London and produce *The Miracle* at Olympia, with a cast of 2,000 – and an audience of 20,000.

And in the same month, back in Berlin, he created his production of *Everyman*, the play to which he was going to find himself tied for most of the rest of his life.

*

By this time he had begun to construct a lifestyle on a scale worthy of the productions he was doing. He was surrounded by a court of advisers, assistants, hangers-on, and indigent relatives whom he had put on the payroll; he had a series of women; he dressed with fastidious elegance and ate only in the best restaurants; when he travelled he did it in the style of a prince on the Grand Tour. What all this cost he had not the slightest idea – his money was managed for him by his chamberlain, his depressive brother Edmund, whom he had rescued from suicide (and whom Helene Thimig thought was the greatest love of his life). He was, it was often said, a baroque figure. It was the opportunity of acquiring a baroque palace at a knock-down price in the great inflation after the First World War that brought him back to Salzburg, where he had begun his theatrical career a quarter of a century earlier with a single suitcase in a single room.

*Le style est l'homme même*, said the Comte de Buffon, and it is surely true that in any human being it is difficult to make a distinction between the man himself and his outward expression in deeds and a way of being. In Reinhardt's case, though, the inner source of all that energy, achievement and display seems particularly elusive. 'Rarely,' said Heinz Herald, one of his associates over many years, 'has a human being remained so anonymous to those close to him, or has been revealed so totally in his work, as Reinhardt.' Another of his associates, the Austrian playwright Hermann Bahr, wrote: 'Paradoxically one could say of Reinhardt that the real charm of his personality consisted of his having none.' He had, said his son Gottfried, 'a reticence touching on the pathological . . . His paralysing reaction to direct contact with people, his inability to communicate with them freely, is indicative of the dark pockets in his soul.'

He often seemed to inhabit his vast carapace as thinly as a night-watchman in an empty warehouse. He was a legendary host (particularly at Leopoldskron), and, according to Helene Thimig, 'he loved big gatherings – but only to look at. He was mad to have people around him – but he was desperate at being alone with individual people.' He was charismatic, persuasive and articulate when he was dealing with actors, writers and people whose support he needed. But outside his professional life it was different. Thimig said 'he found it extremely unpleasant to talk *tête-à-tête*, particularly in a separate space cut off from the company. He never knew what to say.' Reinhardt said of himself that he found it difficult to breathe except in 'the true unreality of the theatre'.

It is impossible to know whether he consciously recognised any parallel between himself and Everyman, the eponymous protagonist of the play to which he now found himself yoked. I can find no record of his saying anything to this effect. So far as I know he had not intended to revisit the piece after its outing in Berlin, where it had had a poor reception from the critics (though a warm one from the public). For the opening of the first Salzburg Festival, in 1920, he had commissioned a young Austrian writer, Max Mell, to provide him with a modern mystery play about his future heroine the Virgin Mary, in Salzburg dialect. But it was not ready in time, and he fell back on the nearest equivalent to hand, the *Everyman* that he had done in Berlin nine years earlier. Would a play in Salzburgerisch rather than High German have caught on as *Everyman* now did? Many other plays were performed in the festival seasons that followed (some of them, including a suitably gigantic *Faust*, directed by Reinhardt himself). But it

was *Everyman* that became its emblem. Reinhardt revived it
every summer (apart from a couple of years in the twenties)
until the Nazis came to power in 1938, and drove both him and
the play into exile. It resumed its career and its emblematic
status at Salzburg after the Nazis (and Reinhardt) had gone,
and has now outlived him by over sixty years.

The play is by Hugo von Hofmannsthal, whose long
collaboration with Reinhardt had begun with his version of
*Oedipus*. Hofmannsthal derived it from an English morality play
of the fifteenth century, *The Summoning of Everyman*, and it has a
simple plot. God, outraged by the indifference and ingratitude
of mankind, sends Death to summon Everyman to judgment.
Everyman, suitably terrified, repents of his past failings,
abandons his worldly possessions, proclaims his faith, and is
welcomed into heaven, apparently redeemed.

How God, or Death, selects the individual who is to serve
as an exemplar of humankind at large is not clear. The victim
they hit upon between them, well suited as he is to be a
popular target for retribution, is no more an average citizen
than Reinhardt was. Like Reinhardt he is wealthy and rejoices
in it. He lives in a grand house, and receives his unexpected
summons during the course of a sumptuous banquet he is
giving for his mistress and troops of friends. (He even seems
to have some of Reinhardt's social inhibitions – his mistress
has to urge him to join his guests.) At this point in the play,
however, and at the point in Reinhardt's career when he first
produced it, their paths diverge. As soon as they discover the
identity of Everyman's visitor, and the nature of the journey
he has been summoned to make, his mistress, friends, and
servants all desert him, and he can derive neither help nor
comfort from his wealth. Reinhardt had another eighteen
years to enjoy his worldly substance and the company of his
associates.

The English original now seems archaic and inaccessible.
One of its modern editors says that it 'was written in the
interests of the established faith; to uphold the papal authority;
to emphasise the claims of the priesthood; to insist on the
efficacy of the sacraments.' Another editor detects the hand
of a priest in its construction, and the dramatic focus is plainly

on Everyman's redemption. Hofmannsthal, a real dramatist (probably best-known outside Germany or his native Austria as the author of most of Richard Strauss's libretti, beginning with the magnificent *Rosenkavalier* – the first production of which, at Dresden in 1911, Reinhardt directed), has made it dramatically viable. One of the many things he has modified is the play's theology. The original is presumably among other things a contribution to the long-running debate about the relative importance of faith and works, and Good Works is the only one of the various personified virtues and faculties around Everyman who stands by him, and who single-handedly makes his redemption possible. Hofmannsthal has introduced the figure of Faith, and given her an equal role in Everyman's salvation.

Even in Hofmannsthal's version this aspect of the play is difficult for the non-believer to take much interest in – or to make much sense of. A faith hastily rediscovered under sentence of death and threat of eternal hellfire is surely as dubious as a confession obtained by torture. Good Works (or, as Hofmannsthal calls her, simply Works) is an even more curious figure. When we first meet her she is in a bad way as a result of Everyman's lifelong neglect – 'cold in the ground', in the original, 'pitifully weak' in Hofmannsthal – and unable to stir. How she regains her strength retrospectively, when she enters the story too late for Everyman to undertake any addition to his achievements in life, or any modification of them, it's difficult to understand. The moral would seem to be that there's no need to bother with behaving well, because you can always rewrite the record afterwards.

The strength of the piece now is its dramatisation of the unpredictability and inexorability of the end that waits for all of us, believers and non-believers alike. Any doubts I had about whether Hofmannsthal's handling of this could still be effective were abruptly shattered by seeing a DVD of Christian Stückl's production of the play at the 2004 Festival, with Peter Simonischek as a big, powerful, likeable, immensely human Everyman, caught in the rich fullness of his life by Jenz Harzer as a naked, grey-fleshed, burning-eyed Death. Even on the small screen it is an unforgettable experience.

In spite of the play's enduring power, and the success it had
in Salzburg, the audience it found was not the one that
Reinhardt had been aiming at. Ordinary local citizens didn't
much like it, and in any case they couldn't afford the ticket
prices. The customers (as always) turned out to be the rich and
the tourists. Franz Rehrl, the Provincial Governor, was a strong
supporter of the Festival – but for purely hard-headed reasons.
'Culture,' he said, 'equals business.' Not even the business,
though, reconciled the intensely conservative citizens of Salzburg
to the influx of the outsiders who brought it to them. One of
these outsiders, of course, was Reinhardt himself. 'Philistines
in Salzburg,' wrote Hofmannsthal to Richard Strauss in 1923,
'will never accept Reinhardt as president [of the Festival].
They hate him as a Jew, as a Lord of the Manor, as an artist
and as a solitary human being whom they cannot fathom.'
The tinge of anti-Semitism in local resentment was strong, and
the most outspoken opponents of the Festival were the local
forerunners of the Nazis. Already contemptuous of Catholicism
as practised by Catholics, they were even more virulent about
the 'hypocritical profit-Catholicism of Jews', among whom
they included not only Reinhardt but Hofmannsthal, the
Catholic grandson of a Jewish convert. Reinhardt was also
a permanent target for the Viennese satirist Karl Kraus, still
widely admired in *bien-pensant* circles today, who described him,
with a wonderful combination of racial and social disdain, as
'an upstart from the Slovak working class'.

Leopoldskron, too, turned out not to be the quiet artistic
and intellectual cloister that Reinhardt had envisaged. It
became inevitable, said Thimig later, to invite politicians and
money as well. 'Particularly unpleasant,' she says, 'I found the
representatives of the so-called "entertainment aristocracy".'
Money (as always) came to dominate the Festival, like Mammon
springing out of Everyman's trunk. At first everyone involved
in the play worked for nothing. But as the seasons went by the
well-known actors who came to Salzburg began to demand the
kind of fees they could command elsewhere. The Festival
accumulated a considerable deficit, and not even high ticket
prices could keep it afloat. It seems to have been rescued by
a millionaire, Camillo Castiglioni, who had amassed a fortune

building planes during the First World War and speculating in the great inflation that followed it (and another Jew, like so many of the philanthropists who keep the arts going).

So poor Everyman had to be preserved by the very wealth that had failed to sustain him in the play, and redeemed at the expense of patrons who did not believe in Christian redemption. It sounds more and more like the situation in the British (and the German) theatre today, which struggles piously to present plays about poverty and degradation to an audience not very closely acquainted with either – and which has to be subsidised by the charitable efforts of people on even more remote terms with them.

Well, perhaps they learn a few things that they didn't know, and are persuaded to go out and give all they have to the poor. Perhaps the audience of *Everyman* were moved to make some early improvements to the Good Works section of their CVs. It certainly seems to have spoken to the Prince Archbishop of Salzburg. Gusti Adler, in her biography of Reinhardt, reports that at the first performance quiet tears rolled down his cheeks, and that when he pressed Reinhardt's hand afterwards he said that the production was better than a sermon. But then, according to Reinhardt, he was a saint anyway.

It's difficult to know about the rest of the audience. Reinhardt himself certainly didn't change his lifestyle. Is that a criticism of the play? Of the production? Of Reinhardt? He may of course have felt that if the Deutsches Theater and *Everyman* counted for anything, his record of Works was strong enough to counterbalance quite a lot of champagne and cigars. And Hofmannsthal was certainly right about the terrifying unpredictability of death. In 1929 his elder son shot himself, and Hofmannsthal himself died of a heart attack as he dressed for the funeral. Three days later the same unannounced visitor came for Reinhardt's beloved brother Edmund.

\*

My play, like two earlier ones of mine, *Copenhagen* and *Democracy*, is based on the historical record, but perhaps rather more freely than they were.

Reinhardt himself, elusive and unforthcoming as his associates often found him, was in his letters and other writings immensely articulate, eloquent, sophisticated and prolific. Most of the ideas that he expresses in the play are drawn from what he wrote, but I have not even begun to do justice to the depth of his intelligence or the breadth of his culture. The external events of his life – his difficulties with local philistines and anti-Semites, the attacks on his house (and on the Prince Archbishop's), his expropriation and exile – are drawn from the record. And from the terrace of Leopoldskron you can indeed see Obersalzberg, above Berchtesgaden on the other side of the German frontier, where Hitler and other Nazi leaders had their villas.

Reinhardt's recollections of his childhood in Vienna and of his first arrival in Salzburg come mostly from his autobiographical notes. His working methods are described not only here but in the recollections of many professional colleagues, and also in three full-length memoirs – by his second wife Helene Thimig, by his personal assistant Gusti Adler, and by his younger son Gottfried. These are also the source for most of the details of his personal life – his relations with his brother Edmund, his efforts to support the rest of his extended family, the difficulties with his first wife, his princely travel arrangements, and his accommodation in Berlin and Vienna; for his distaste for handling or thinking about money, and his financial difficulties in exile, including his emergency cash arrangements (though he did have one success during his bleak American exile – *Rosalinda*, an adaptation of *Die Fledermaus* – which was produced in New York in 1942, and which just about kept him afloat); for his legendary parties; for his deferential consultation with Rothschild and other patrons; for his unfulfilled projects to commission a play from Shaw about the life of Christ and to film *Paradise Lost*.

Gottfried's memoirs (which he wrote in English) are particularly revealing, if somewhat overblown in style. His love for his father, reverence for his talent, and encylopaedic knowledge of his affairs (in every sense) do not impede him from casting a coolly observant eye upon his manifold weaknesses. Reinhardt, he says, was 'a precocious, hypersensitive,

fantasy-possessed, play-mad, cruel-tender child to whom
tenderness from others was as necessary as food and drink . . .
an enthusiast and a skeptic, courageous and quickly intimidated,
a gambler and an evader of decision, at one time trusting
providence, at another taking refuge in procrastination,
immune to fatal catastrophe, but an easy prey to the most
banal mishap . . . '

The character of Rudolf Kommer, Reinhardt's man of
business and master of ceremonies, is also very fully documented
by Gottfried, including his division of the human race into the
imposters and the feeble-minded. Gottfried says he 'played
confidant, counsellor, caretaker, father confessor, procurer,
arbiter, entertainer, to the international upper crust'. He was
a kind of eunuch, continuously but harmlessly in love with
a harem of other people's wives and girlfriends, whom he
entertained and consoled, and who all called him Kätchen in
affectionate gratitude. The guests at one of Reinhardt's great
parties, says Gottfried, would find themselves . . .

> staring in surprise at a person who happened to be in their midst
> as if by accident and who chatted nonchalantly and without ever
> stopping. He chatted with the virtuoso brilliance of a pianist,
> eliciting complicated cadences from the keys without seeming to
> touch them. He would turn from one to the other, called most by
> their first names and acted with such ease that one would think
> this centrifugal mass of people, alien and feeling alienated, were the
> oldest acquaintances and had simply run into one another again,
> and that he was continuing a conversation long since begun . . .
>
> There was no spoilsport who did not start to grin at the sight of
> him. He was the heart of the whole company and pumped blood
> even into its stiffest and most congealed members. He entertained
> and found entertainment in everybody. He formed friendship
> upon friendship and quarrelled with some to the point of physical
> violence, without, however, extinguishing his cigarette or his wit.
> He spiced the fat life of the rich with sharp truths, gave away
> boxes of candy, flowers and books, lunched, dined, supped
> (sometimes in repetition with first and second understudies), he
> debated, talked politics, criticised without surcease and, when he
> failed to incur enough contradictions, he started contradicting

himself. He arranged divorces for excitable men, married off
women, played with their children, concluded agreements between
producers, poets, directors, musicians . . .

At night, in the bar, he could make Jews yodel, Nazis *jüdeln* [talk
with a Jewish inflection] . . . Without the slightest condescension,
he could make every servant his friend and disarm every enemy
with the perfect gallantry of a born aristocrat . . .

At the end of their long collaboration Reinhardt and Kommer
became estranged from each other, though it's difficult to
establish exactly how and why. According to Gottfried,
Kommer wrote a long letter to Reinhardt 'enumerating, in
Kommer's opinion, every error my father had ever committed
and complaining about my father's ingratitude for his services'.
Reinhardt responded with a farewell letter 56 pages long in
which he gave a brilliant and generous account of Kommer's
career and character, largely in the third person.

The originals of the other characters are somewhat less well
documented. Gusti Adler was the niece of Victor Adler, the
founder of the Austrian Social Democratic Party, and an old
school friend of Thimig's. She had started out in life studying
art, and then become a cultural journalist. She worked round
the clock for Reinhardt, says Thimig, and did everything for
him, including buying rare books and antiques, and rare
animals and exotic birds for the garden; the only thing she
couldn't fix was the Salzburg weather. From her own book
she emerges as devoted and totally uncritical.

Thimig, on the evidence of *her* memoir, was a little more
detached. She came from a famous Viennese acting family,
and had a successful stage career of her own. She fully shared
Reinhardt's passion for restoring and furnishing Leopoldskron,
but never, she says, a double bedroom, except in the bug-ridden
hotel on the Mexican border where they were establishing
their immigration into the United States as a preliminary to his
getting a divorce in Reno from his first wife. Even on their
train journeys between New York and Los Angeles they had
a drawing-room suite with separate bedrooms. She is frank
about the jealousy that she felt for some of the women who
were drawn to Reinhardt – particularly Lady Diana Cooper,

his Nun and Virgin, and Eleonora von Mendelssohn, the
wealthy, beautiful (and drug-addicted) socialite who was closer
to Reinhardt than she was herself in the last painful weeks of
his life. She is (fairly) frank, too, about the triangle that
developed when she herself fell for the actor she was working
with in a romantic comedy.

The Prince Archbishop of Salzburg, Dr Ignatius Rieder,
seems to have been admired and loved by everyone (except
by the Nazis, and perhaps by the droves of people who were
leaving the church at that time to join them). He was profoundly
conservative in demeanour and outlook, and maintained
contacts with the imperial family even after the dissolution of
the Dual Monarchy in 1918. Thimig describes him as having a
peasant's face capped by snow-white hair, and always wearing
a peasant's heavy boots. She found him particularly noble and
good; Reinhardt described him as a saint, and as 'the angelic
archbishop'. The Archbishop reciprocated. 'A good Jew like
Reinhardt,' he said, 'is dearer to me than a bad Christian' –
a sentiment that would perhaps sound platitudinous in a
churchman now, but that was not to be taken quite so much for
granted in Salzburg at the time. He was one of the relatively
few people in Salzburg who were enthusiastic about the Festival,
and he gave Reinhardt permission to perform *Everyman* in front
of the cathedral. (Reinhardt put his request in a letter; the
reading of the play in support of the application is my expansion
of this.) The two men developed a warm personal relationship.
Thimig says that the Archbishop discreetly blessed Leopoldskron
for them, in spite of its being a Jewish home, and she describes
how he would sometimes tenderly stroke Reinhardt's arm and
call him 'my son'.

Franz, Reinhardt's valet, has a slightly more oblique
relationship to reality. The real Franz had, like mine, previously
been valet to Luziwuzi, the transvestite Archduke Ludwig
Viktor, who had caused much embarrassment to his brother
the Emperor. (Franz's job description in his earlier post was not
only valet but *Vorleser* – 'reader aloud' – though what he read
I have been unable to discover.) But at some point, I think in
the 1930s, Death came for Franz and he was replaced by Paul.
Reinhardt retained Paul's services throughout the bleak years

of American exile, even though he was often unable to pay
him, which Paul seems to have been rather less sanguine about
than my character. I have elided Paul with Franz.

Friedrich Müller is a degree more fictitious. He is based on
a man called Friedrich Rainer, who shared with my character
many of the political and racist views that were common at the
time in Salzburg, as elsewhere in Austria, and who, like Müller,
joined the Nazi Party and went into local politics. I changed
his name partly because 'Rainer' sounds confusingly like
'Reinhardt', but also because Rainer grew up not in Salzburg
but in Sankt Veit, and because it was not Rainer who conveyed
to Reinhardt Hitler's bizarre offer of rebirth as an honorary
Aryan.

This is an event doubted by some but confirmed by both
Thimig and Adler, who agree that the messenger was Death
himself. Or, at any rate, Werner Krauss, the actor who played
the part for many years in *Everyman*, and who was also an
outspoken Nazi supporter. Reinhardt was particularly fond
of him. He had made his name in 1920, in *The Cabinet of Dr
Caligari*, but during the thirties he specialised in playing Jews
in Nazi propaganda films. In 1933 Reinhardt cast him as
Mephistopheles in his Salzburg *Faust* after he had agreed to
sack the original casting, Max Pallenberg, because he was
Jewish.

Müller's history, however, coincides closely with Rainer's
after the Anschluss in 1938, when Hitler appointed Rainer
Gauleiter of Salzburg. Up to then Rainer had called for the
unconditional destruction of everything Catholic and Jewish
in Salzburg. He now decided to preserve all the decadent
baroque Catholic trappings of Leopoldskron – and to move
into the house himself. During the war he continued his rise
through the ranks of the Nazi administration, and ended up in
charge of Friuli, the Italian province on the Yugoslav border.
After the war he appeared as a witness at Nuremberg before
being handed over to the Yugoslavs and hanged at Ljubljana
in 1947 (though rumours persisted, as with other executed war
criminals, that he had somehow survived).

*

My translations of the extracts from Hofmannsthal's text are fairly free, but I hope reflect something of the dramatic quality of the original. I have been pretty cavalier in my selection, taking only what suits my purposes, occasionally slightly changing the order of events, and skipping completely the sections dealing with Everyman's redemption. Hofmannsthal's text is written mostly in iambic tetrameters, but with occasionally longer or shorter lines, and rhymed mostly as couplets, though he often varies this, so far as I can see randomly. Since I was using only short extracts which needed to be clearly distinguished from their prose background I thought that I should stick strictly to regular tetrameters and regular couplets.

I feel uneasy about taking such liberties with a writer as good as Hofmannsthal. I can only say in justification that Hofmannsthal himself has made very free with his sources. The English text on which he has drawn, which may itself be taken from a Dutch original, is written in verse so irregular that its prosody is almost unfollowable. He has also heavily recast it, cutting among other characters Strength, Discretion, Five-wits, Beauty, Knowledge and Confession, and adding some dozen new ones. He has reshaped the action and made it genuinely dramatic, and changed the whole theological basis of the play by introducing the character of Faith. His German editor Heinz Rölleke identifies material imported from completely different sources, some of them highly anachronistic – a rhymed prayer of Dürer's, songs from the Minnesingers, and scenes from Calderon and Maeterlinck. He has also, says Rölleke, drawn on Burton's *The Anatomy of Melancholy* for Everyman's character and on the nineteenth-century German sociologist Georg Simmel for Everyman's and Mammon's philosophy of money (both of which I have quoted at length).

I have taken further liberties with names and titles. Actors often called Reinhardt 'Max', but this was a collegial informality, and Thimig says that she always referred to him as 'Reinhardt'. Even this was a wifely intimacy, though, and to most people he was 'Professor Reinhardt', an honorary designation bestowed upon him by the Duke of Saxonia-Coburg-Gotha; Austrians are notoriously meticulous about titles ('Doktor Doktor', for example, if you have two doctorates) – and open-handed about creating fictitious ones for citizens unfortunate enough not to possess real titles. Aristocratic ranks were abolished in 1918, but the old titles that went with them often continued to be used, and waiters in Viennese coffee houses are said to call any unfamiliar customer 'Herr Baron' or 'Herr Direktor'. One of the reasons that Thimig was so anxious to get married to Reinhardt, says his son acidly, was to be addressed as 'Frau Professor'. In America he apparently became 'Doctor', but in English these usages applied to a theatre director sound – to my ears, at any rate – so odd and egregious that I have left him as plain Herr Reinhardt.

He usually referred to Thimig, she says, as 'die Leni' – a characteristically Germanic usage that suggests both familiarity and respect, and that has no equivalent in English. To other people at that time, before her marriage to Reinhardt, she and Adler would have been 'gnädiges Fräulein' – gracious Miss – but a simple 'Fräulein' is the nearest approximation that sounds reasonable in English. Most of the references I have found to Dr Rieder, both at the time and since, call him *Fürsterzbischof*, Prince Archbishop, and when Reinhardt wrote to him he began his letter 'Eurer fürstlichen Gnaden' – Your Princely Grace. This is really another 'Herr Baron'. The last real Prince Archbishop of Salzburg was Hieronymus von Colloredo, whose tenure ended in 1812, by which time the office had been stripped of its temporal powers, so that all Colloredo's successors have been plain ordinary archbishops. Until the 1940s, though, they were still addressed as princes.

*

Real death is rarely the tidy and dignified event suggested by the mythic representation of it that forms the basis of Hofmannsthal's play. It wasn't for Hofmannsthal himself, who died still struggling to put his top hat on for his son's funeral. It wasn't for Rudolf Kommer, when he collapsed and died in 1943 in the lobby of his hotel room in New York, where the body had to be left until the coroner could be located – so that all the crowds of acquaintances who came to pay their respects had to step over him to do so.

Nor was it for Reinhardt when it came, slowly, over the course of three weeks and a series of strokes, in another New York hotel room seven months later, apparently after he had been bitten by a dog. Money ruled over his deathbed, as it had over so much of his life; Gottfried hushed up his condition for fear that it would frighten off the investors in the production he was trying to set up (an adaptation of Offenbach's *La Belle Hélène*, intended to follow up the success of *Rosalinda*).

Gusti Adler and Helene Thimig, however, both lived happily ever after – or at any rate for many more years after Reinhardt's death. Adler, who had followed him into exile in 1939, and worked for him unpaid in the evenings while she earned a living from her day job in the archive at Warner Brothers, continued at the studio until she was in her eighties, and lived on into her nineties. Thimig struggled back to Austria in 1946 to play her old role as Faith in *Everyman* at Salzburg, then went on to resume her distinguished stage career in Vienna. For twenty-five years she lived happily with the Austrian actor Anton Edthofer, and died in 1974 at the age of 85.

Reinhardt's renunciation of Leopoldskron, I discovered as my researches continued, was not quite as simple as it seemed in the letter he wrote to his wife in 1942 that was quoted in the brochure. He continued to be profoundly anguished by his loss, and he never gave up the hope of recovering the house. In July the following year, three months before his death, he wrote another letter to his wife, 28 pages long, laying out what seems to be a deposition to an Austrian exile organisation preparing for the post-war restitution of property stolen by the Nazis, in which he attempts to catalogue the contents of the house, to list the improvements and additions that he and his wife have made, together with all the services he has rendered to the Austrian nation, and all the honours and recognition he has received for his work. It is rather like Everyman's account of his estate – but offered after he has lost it, in the hope that Death might relent, and return it to him. Death did not oblige, any more than it did for Everyman.

It was, however, after endless legal difficulties and battles, returned to his heirs – his wife and sons, who sold it to the American academic organisation that runs it today. And there it still stands, in all its lofty baroque elegance. The great impresario has gone, and so have the princes and financiers who were his guests, together with the actors and musicians who entertained them, and the thieves and murderers who followed them. Now the guests drifting elegantly about the marble hall and the terrace are a new privileged class – the conference-goers of the world. You can rent its facilities yourself when the Seminar is not in session.

And in its afterlife it has achieved a certain celebrity through its artistic associations – even become a place of pilgrimage that attracts coach parties from all over Europe. Not because of Max Reinhardt, but because it served as a location in the film version of *The Sound of Music*.

# SOURCES

## Biography

Leonhard M. Fiedler: *Max Reinhardt* (1975).

## Personal memoirs

Helene Thimig-Reinhardt: *Wie Max Reinhardt Lebte* (1973).

Gusti Adler: . . . *aber vergessen Sie nicht die chinesischen Nachtigallen* (1980, but expanded from *Max Reinhardt – sein Leben*, 1964). The title of the 1980 edition refers to Reinhardt's reminder to Adler, as she left Leopoldskron to meet Lilian Gish off the boat from New York at Cuxhaven. She was to stop off on the way at Hagenbeck, the animal dealers near Hamburg, to buy flamingos, pelicans, herons and exotic ducks. 'But don't forget the Chinese nightingales!' he called after her.

Gottfried Reinhardt: *The Genius, a Memoir of Max Reinhardt* (1979). In English.

## Reinhardt's own writings

Max Reinhardt: *Manuskripte, Briefe, Dokumente* (1998). The catalogue of a collection made by Dr Jürgen Stein, but with many quoted extracts.

Max Reinhardt: *Ich bin nichts als ein Theatermann* (1974 in the DDR, 1989 in the BRD). A collection of his letters about theatrical matters, together with brief memoirs by some of his associates.

## The story of the house and the Festival

Johannes Hofinger: *Die Akte Leopoldskron* (2005).

Stephen Gallup: *A History of the Salzburg Festival* (1987). In English.

## Essays and documents

*Ambivalenzen: Max Reinhardt und Österreich* (2004). A collection of press cuttings, other documents and photographs.

Roland Koberg, Bernd Stegemann, Henrike Thomsen, eds: *Max Reinhardt und das Deutsche Theater* (2005). Essays, including a particularly interesting one by Christopher Balme, 'Die Marke Reinhardt', on Reinhardt's theatre considered as a business enterprise.